When I first heard about Bob's *Marketing Dictionary for the 21ˢᵗ Century*, I thought, "Great! This will be a wonderful resource for the copywriting classes I teach." I frequently need concise definitions or key concepts in my classes or articles. This book fills the bill on that account. But when I looked closely at the book, I realized it's much more than a dictionary. It's truly a complete overview of every aspect of marketing condensed to bite-sized chunks. Bob's book must be on every marketer's, copywriter's, and advertising person's bookshelf.

Will Newman, Copywriter, Copywriting Instructor

Bob, you had me at "Aggregation"! By the time I was only half way through the "A's" I knew this book was a "must have" resource for anyone who is or strives to be a direct response marketer. This book will absolutely give all entrepreneurs, business owners and marketers a competitive edge.

MaryEllen Tribby, Best selling author, *Reinventing The Entrepreneurs: Turning Your Dream Business into a Reality,* Founder WorkingMomsOnly.com

Paging through Bob Bly's *Marketing Dictionary for the 21ˢᵗ Century* provides a marketing education in itself, as well as serving as a useful reference for the novice and professional marketer alike. I learned a lot just by turning the pages and scanning this book. Very useful.

Mark Ferguson, Numisma Publishing

Bob, I've been reading and actually doing direct marketing my whole career, to my surprise I still found this really helpful, there were so many terms I didn't know and I even picked up a great marketing idea for a new project by learning something new.

Thanks **B**ob!

Blake Houser, Client Relations Manager

Bob's Marketing Dictionary is a great tool to quickly understand the constantly evolving Marketing Slang used in our industry. Now that I have it, I know it will save me time and spare me any confusion when dealing with partners and contractors.

Andrew Contreras, Athletic Greens

Like a carpenter or any other workman, a marketer uses specific and exact tools. When you know all the tools at your disposal... you can solve marketing problems much more quickly and easily. You're not using the handle of a screwdriver to drive nails into wet concrete! *The Marketing Dictionary for the 21ˢᵗ Century* explains these tools in a clear and understandable way. Opening the door to more successful marketing programs - and better communication with co-workers and managers who may not be 'tech savvy' themselves.

Jesse Barton, Bridge Publications

This is the most comprehensive marketing dictionary I've ever seen, and it is long overdue.

Jerry Montgomery, CEO, 5W Strategists, Inc.

Bob has once again delivered a great book to help marketers become more successful in their day-to-day projects. I have been following Bob's work since I read his excellent, *The Copywriter's Handbook: A Step-By-Step Guide To Writing Copy That Sells. The Marketing Dictionary for the 21ˢᵗ Century* contains a wealth of easy-to-understand marketing term definitions, which will come in handy to anyone in marketing, from entry-level to seasoned marketing professionals. Just look up some of those definitions, insert them in your next conversation about a marketing topic, and you will look sharp as a whistle! This broad marketing dictionary, which also includes definitions of the latest marketing-related technology terms, is a must-have in every marketing professional library.

Aliona Groh, Marketing Analyst – Digital Media, Embraer Executive Jets

Marketing Dictionary for the 21st Century

Second Edition

Robert W. Bly

AUTHORS PLACE
—PRESS—

Published by Authors Place Press
9885 Wyecliff Drive, Suite 200
Highlands Ranch, CO 80126
Authorsplace.com

Manufactured in the United States of America.

ISBN: 978-1-62865-826-2

Contents

Testimonials 1

Acknowledgments 8

Introduction 9

Marketing Dictionary for the 21st Century 11

Bibliography 199

About the author 200

For Tiffany Volpe

Acknowledgments

I thank Tony Ferraro, Janie Watanabe, Teri Whitten, and the entire publishing team at Authors Place Press for sharing my enthusiasm for this dictionary and for all the fun I had doing it. Seldom have I enjoyed a book project more! Thanks also to Ilise Benun for suggesting many additional terms not in my first draft. And thanks to those who contributed ideas or terms including Eunice Dean, Bradley Irvine, Ron Schmidt, Shamus Brown, Mele Williams, Scott Martin, Dave Ryan, Penny Hunt, Steve Jolly, Louis Wasser, Ryan Healy, Gordon Graham, Richard Armstrong, Jack LaRue, Daniel Taylor, Paul Black, Len Bailey, Udo from Germany, and others I apologize to for failing to name here.

Several reference works served as sources for definitions, including *Heidelberg's Glossary of Printing Terms, Honeycomb Direct Mail Tips and Resources, Creative Commons Glossary of Internet Marketing Techie-Terms, Glossary of Marketing Definitions* by Dr. Christine Koontz, Matthew Woodward's *Internet Marketing & SEO Jargon Buster,* Association of Advertisers in Ireland *Glossary of Advertising Terms,* IAB Interactive *Advertising Wiki Glossary,* Barron's *Dictionary of Marketing Terms, Oxford Dictionary of Marketing, Successful Direct Marketing Methods* by Bob Stone and Ron Jacobs, *Internet Marketing Dictionary* by Tim and Chris Beachum, and The Ultimate List of Digital Marketing Glossary Terms, https://blog.flightmedia.co/marketing-sales-terms-everyone-know.

Introduction

Thanks largely to several factors – mainly the advent of the internet, the dominance of mobile technology, the proliferation of marketing channels, the rise of social media, the evolution of content marketing, the benefits of list segmentation, the growth of Big Data, better and faster web analytics, artificial intelligence, and the ever-widening behavioral gap between the Baby Boomers and the Millennials – marketing is evolving at an unprecedented pace, making many marketing dictionaries obsolete. To keep you current with important new developments, tactics, concepts, and terms in modern marketing, we have published our Second Edition of the *Marketing Dictionary for the 21st Century*, the book you now hold in your hands.

We believe the *Marketing Dictionary for the 21st Century: Second Edition* is the most contemporary, up-to-date, and authoritative glossary of marketing terms on the market today. One reason is that the author is not just a professor or book author, but an active practitioner who has been deeply involved in marketing for more than four decades. During this time, I have continued to hone my craft and expand my marketing knowledge – experience and information that help make this dictionary up-to-date, specific, and practical. But in my past life, I was an adjunct marketing professor at New York University. And I have given marketing seminars all over the world. So, I have a strong sense of what marketers need and want to know about the "new marketing" – and have honed ways to explain these notions in clear, simple, nontechnical language.

My youngest son asked why I would bother to write, and why anyone would bother to read, my dictionary of marketing terms. I explained that while many dictionary writers are academics and scholars, my real-world experience with the hundreds of marketing tactics, methods, and channels in this book, both offline and online, adds depth and dimension to the definitions that many other dictionaries lack.

This new dictionary contains concepts – such as the core buying complex and dominant resident emotion – not typically found in marketing dictionaries and reference books. Not just theoretical, the definitions include examples from real-life multichannel marketing campaigns conducted by the author, his clients, and many other marketers.

I do have a favor to ask. If you know of a term we have omitted, please let me know so I can include it in the next edition. You can reach me at:

Bob Bly
Copywriter
31 Cheyenne Drive
Montville, NJ 07045
Phone: 973-263-0562
Fax: 973-263-0613
Email: rwbly@bly.com
Website: www.bly.com

A

A/B split test – Testing two different versions of a promotion to see which generates the most responses. Some marketers like to split test two completely different promotions to find a winner. Others test two versions of the same promotion, altering only one variable, such as the headline, product price, offer, size of the mailer, color, or some other key element. Testing tells you what works best for the variable tested; for instance, do landing pages perform better when the headline is in red type or blue?

Abandon rate – The percentage of website visitors who start to fill out the shopping cart but do not complete it or submit an order. A high abandon rate often correlates with a poorly designed shopping cart.

Above the fold – The portion of a web page or email you see when you open it on the screen. The rest, which you have to scroll down to view, is considered below the fold.

Above the line advertising – Creative advertising campaigns usually done by major consumer brands and Madison Avenue ad agencies to promote a brand rather than generate direct sales.

Accordion fold – Folding a legal-size or larger piece of paper at least twice vertically to make multiple panels. Used mainly for brochures and self-mailers. When opened, it unfolds like an accordion to reveal the panels inside.

Account – An advertising agency's client. An account may be an entire corporation or just divisions or segments of it. And for that client, the agency may handle all marketing or just certain aspects of it, with the other tasks done in-house or by other ad agencies with whom they share the account.

Accountability – When the marketing department has to demonstrate a good ROI from their campaigns to senior management.

Account executive (AE) – An advertising agency employee who serves as the liaison between the agency and the client. Account executives play different roles depending on the agency, client, and the AE's personality and skills. In one agency I hired, our account executive was mostly a glad-hander and liaison between me and the agency's creative and media departments; his key talent was going out to lunch. Other AEs play a more substantial role, from formulating marketing plans and advertising schedules to helping the client create new ad campaigns.

Acquisition cost – Amount of money spent on marketing to acquire a new customer.

ACORN – A system of classifying prospects in a residential neighborhood according to location and demographics based on census data.

Acquisition mailing – A direct mail package sent to prospects to convert them into first-time members, customers, donors, or subscribers.

Active customer – A customer who has made a purchase from you recently; e.g., within the last 12 months.

Adaptive creative – The process of determining user purchase intent based on the subject matter of the content the user is currently reading at the moment; this may be more accurate than targeting based on previous content browsed and viewed.[1]

Adobe Acrobat – Free software you can download from Adobe that lets you open and read PDF files.

AdSense – A program in which Google selectively places relevant ads on your website; you as the site owner get a small commission on orders generated by those ads. You do not get to choose which products are featured on your site; Google does the selection automatically via algorithm.

Ad spend – The amount of money spent, usually in one year, on advertising by medium, channel, industry, or company.

Advertising – Paying to have your message published in a specific medium; e.g., buying a full page in the Wall Street Journal or a text ad in an e-newsletter.

---

1   ANA Business Marketing SmartBrief, 8/4/2021.

Advertising network – A group of websites in which the advertising is controlled by a single online publisher or marketer. Your ads will appear on various sites in the ad network at various times. You make more impressions than just advertising on a single site that is not part of a network.

Advertisement – A paid message in which the sponsor or advertiser is identified. Because the ad is a paid message, the advertiser largely controls the content and design within the limits specified by the publication or other medium in which he is buying the ad. For instance, when doing a text ad in an online newsletter, the publisher gives a maximum word length or character count that the ad cannot exceed.

Ad blocker – Software that prevents online ads from being displayed on the user's screen.

Ad clicks – Number of times users click on an ad banner.

Ad views (impressions) – Number of times an ad banner is downloaded and presumably seen by visitors.

Add-on pricing – Charges over and above the base price, typically shipping, handling, and sales tax.

Address – A unique identifier for a computer or site online, usually a URL for a Website or marked with a @ for an email address.

Ad tracker – Software that tracks response and orders from your online advertising.

Advance renewal – A renewal mailing for a newsletter or magazine sent before the publisher's regular renewal series begins. Advance renewals typically offer a discount, extra issues, or premium that the regular renewal series does not.

Advertising agency – A company that creates and manages advertising campaigns on behalf of its clients.

Advertising allowance – Money given by a manufacturer to the merchants who carry the product to fund the merchant's advertising of that product.

Advertising manager – A professional employed by an advertiser to coordinate and manage the company's advertising program.

Advertorial – An advertisement that reads and often looks like editorial matter – in other words, like an article. But its purpose is to promote a product. Unlike native advertising, which in appearance mimics an ad, the advertorial can be designed either like an article or an ad. The advertorial seems like it is journalism but, actually, it is promotion.

Advertising specialty – A promotional item given to prospects and customers by a marketer, usually imprinted with the marketer's logo and name.

Aerial advertising – An ad message on the side of a blimp or on a banner trailing an airplane. Today, many aerial advertisements are on smaller blimps operated by remote control. It also refers to promotional banners in the sky and attached to small planes and also to ad messages in skywriting.

Affiliate – Anyone who sells your products online in exchange for a commission you pay them on each sale. Also called an affiliate partner or JV partner.

Affiliate marketing – A system of marketing in which advertiser X sells his product to the e-list or website visitors of advertiser Y. In exchange, advertiser Y gets a commission on every sale ranging from 10 percent to 50 percent of the purchase price. In this case, advertiser X, the product's manufacturer or publisher, would consider advertiser Y, the list owner, as her affiliate. According to the 99/1 rule, 99 percent of your affiliates will account for just one percent of your sales. The reason? Most people who sign up as affiliates are internet marketing amateurs who have tiny lists and no way to sell your product in volumes. That is why you need *super-affiliates* (see definition).

Affiliate program – An arrangement in which a company pays you a percentage of the sale for every online customer they get through a link from your website or emails to theirs. In an **open affiliate program,** anyone and everyone who wants to join can just click a few buttons to sign up. In a **closed affiliate program,** the marketer is selective about whom they accept as affiliates, and potential partners have to ask to be chosen as affiliates.

Affinity – A close relationship with the target group the marketer is trying to reach. Example: owners of sports cars might be targeted by a motorcycle dealership.

Affinity marketing – Marketing efforts – including email promotions, banners, or offline media – aimed at consumers on the basis of established buying patterns or common interests. Example: A company selling a road atlas for RV drivers mails only to members of RV clubs.

Agate line – A unit of measure for space in newspapers and magazines where advertising will run. An agate is 1/14 of an inch high by one column in width.

Agency commission – A 15 percent commission paid to ad agencies that place ads in magazines and newspapers on behalf of the advertisers who are the agency's clients.

Agora Model – Online business model in which you build a large opt-in e-list (also known as your house e-list) and then drive sales by sending solo promotional emails with product offers to your list. The e-list is built by using various traffic generating methods, such as social media and blogging, to drive traffic to a registration page offering a free subscription to an online newsletter.

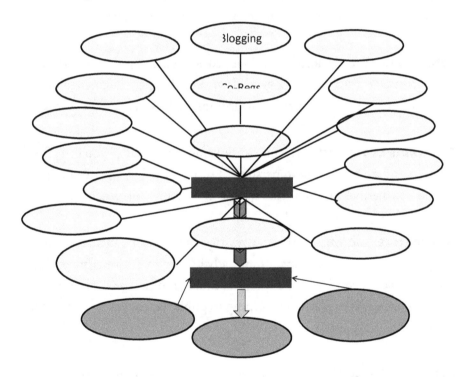

Agora Publishing – A publisher of consumer newsletters credited with inventing the Agora Model.

Aggregation – Market segmentation that assumes most consumers in that segment are alike.

AIDA – A formula for persuasive writing that stands for attention, interest, desire, and ask for the order.

Air time – The amount of actual transmission time on a radio or TV station for running a commercial.

ALT tags – Brief HTML text describing what is in an image when you place your cursor over the image. ALT tags are used so that users whose computers cannot display the image can at least know what picture is in the blank space they are seeing. ALT tags also enable search engines to find and index images on a web page.

Algorithm – A set of formulas developed for the computer to perform a certain task. Facebook, Google, Yahoo, and all other search engines and social media sites are run using algorithms, as does AI and other software.

Allowable order cost – The maximum amount of money you can afford to spend on marketing to persuade a prospect to buy the product; can be based either on the initial sale or the lifetime customer value.

Alternative media – Alternatives to mainstream media such as prime time TV commercials and advertising in national magazines. Example: advertising on paper placemats in diners and placing your business cards in plastic racks hung in public places (such as entrances to diners and restaurants).

AMA (Ask Me Anything) – A webinar for your tribe, subscribers, readers, and fans. In an AMA, there is no specified topic, outline, agenda, or presentation. For 60 to 90 minutes, they can ask you whatever they want to know about, and you answer to the best of your ability. This works best for an audience that has been exposed to some of your ideas and content but wants to know more and would greatly value your answers.

Amazon bestseller campaign – A marketing campaign where you get many marketers with large lists to promote your book on the same day, resulting in enough copies sold that day to drive the book to the number one spot on the Amazon bestseller list. Once popular and effective, now frowned on by Amazon.

Amazon Effect – The Amazon Effect is the ongoing evolution and disruption of the retail market, both online and in physical outlets, resulting from increased e-commerce. The name is an acknowledgment of Amazon's early and continuing domination in online sales, which has driven much of the disruptions, the biggest of which is the ongoing consumer shift from retail to shopping online.[2]

Analytics – Gathering and analyzing data to measure the effectiveness of online marketing as well as consumer behavior on websites. For instance, analytics might show that only 20 percent of visitors enter your site through the home page while 80 percent come into the site through product pages. Analytics track and report on web metrics, which measure performance of various digital marketing activities.

Anchor – A word, phrase, or graphic image; in hypertext, it is the object that is highlighted, underlined, or "clickable" that links to a specific web page.

Announcer – A person who reads radio commercials on the air.

App – A game, software, or content accessible only with a mobile device. Apps for iPhones can be found and downloaded at the iTunes store online. Many apps also run on Android mobile phones.

Appending – Matching your customer files against a national database of businesses or consumers and adding information from those files to your customer records. For instance, all you may know about your

2   https://whatis.techtarget.com/definition/Amazon-effect

B2B customers is the products they bought from you. By running your house file against a national database of businesses, you can locate your customer on that database, find more information on him (e.g., number of offices, email address), and append that information to the customer's record in your house list.

Applet – A small and simple software application.

Application brief – A flier or sheet that explains in detail how a product is used in a specific application. Some products have a wide range of applications, and these are often highlighted in application briefs separate from the main brochure or website.

APP Track Transparency – A feature that enables iPhone users to prevent apps from tracking them.

App, mobile – Applications, such as games, web browsers, calculators, and spreadsheets, accessible through smartphones and other mobile devices. *Native apps* are apps that run exclusively on one specific mobile operating system.

API (application programming interface) – A toolset that programmers can use in helping them create applications software that performs specific functions; e.g., setting alarms, voice recognition, touchscreen activation.

Archiving – To retain email and social media messages that can be retrieved to analyze their effectiveness and also as proof that they comply with advertising laws.

Art director – An ad agency employee responsible for overseeing the graphic design and production of ad layouts.

Art, artwork – A photograph or illustration used in an advertisement.

Artificial Intelligence (AI) – A computer, machine, or software that can mimic certain aspects of human intellect such as image recognition, voice recognition, and reasoning.

Association marketing – Selling your products through and in partnership with an association to its members. Sales increase because the members believe the association is endorsing your products.

ASP (application service provider) – A third-party vendor that develops and hosts internet and intranet applications for consumers.

American Writers and Artists Inc. (AWAI) – A for-profit training company that sells courses, manuals, seminars, and other training on how to make money in freelance copywriting, travel writing, and other writing specialties. In my opinion, AWAI is responsible for transforming freelance copywriting from a small and obscure field into a widely sought-after business opportunity.

Art printing paper – A premium-grade paper stock coated on both sides for the high-quality reproduction of color prints.

Aspect ratio – The ratio between the width and the height of a TV or movie screen; TV commercials must be shot so they fit the aspect ratio. You may notice that some movies on cable TV are modified because they do not fit the aspect ratio of your TV screen.

Attribution – Identifying what ad or other promotion a given click, lead, sale, or other response originated from. In multichannel marketing, the use of a large number of tactics, combined with the difficulty of tracking certain ones in particular (e.g., aerial ads, signage), can make keeping accurate track of attribution a challenge.

Attrition rate – The rate at which customers or prospects leave you. For instance, if you have an email subscriber base of 10,000 and ten people unsubscribe per month, your monthly attrition rate is one-tenth of one percent.

Audience – Total number of consumers reached by a promotion or advertisement.

Audiovisual (A/V) presentation – A presentation involving both pictures and spoken words. TV commercials, slide shows, PowerPoint presentations, online videos, and films are all audiovisual presentations.

Audit bureau – A third-party organization that verifies the subscriber base and readership claimed by a publication, TV or radio station, or other media.

Audit statement – Published results of a bureau's audit to verify a publication's circulation.

Augmented reality (AR) – An environment in which real objects are computer enhanced to add sound, visuals, and other sensory input.

Authority site – A site that is highly respected with great content and a lot of traffic. By getting authority sites to link to your site, you can raise your Google ranking.

Autoplay – An online video that automatically begins to play when you click onto the web page where it is located, rather than requiring the user to click on the video to start it.

Autoresponder – Software that delivers a timed sequence of email marketing messages to prospects who have taken a specific action, such as download a white paper, subscribe to your e-newsletter, or buy a product.

Autoresponder series – The sequence of timed emails delivered by an autoresponder. Each effort in the series is an attempt to get the consumer to buy the product or take another specific action, such as attend a webinar or subscribe to an online newsletter.

Auto-ship – When you are selling a product that gets used up and needs to be replenished (e.g., vitamins, skin cream, diapers, dog food), offer your customers an auto-ship option. In this arrangement, you ship a new supply, often on a monthly schedule, for which you charge their credit card or PayPal account automatically for each shipment. You keep up the automatic monthly shipments until the customer tells you to stop.

Avatar – An idealized representation of an average customer including age, gender, employment, education, income, net worth, and other demographics and psychographics attributed to the ideal customer for your firm.

AVOD (Ad-supported video on demand) – Streaming video services and networks that take paid advertising either instead of or, more commonly, in addition to subscription fees paid by their viewers.

AVS error – An error message sent when a user tries to make a purchase with his credit card in a shopping cart, occurring when the name entered in the shopping cart does not exactly match the name on the card; e.g., if I enter Robert Bly, I will get an AVS message because my card says Robert W. Bly.

Awareness – How well people in your target market are aware of your brand and understand what it is about.

B

B&W – Black and white.

Baby Boomer – Anyone born between 1946 and 1964.

Back-end – Additional sales made to consumers after they become customers by purchasing their first product from you.

Backlink – Links from other websites pointing back to your site. If these links are from sites the search engines see as authoritative and legitimate, the back links will help raise your site's search engine ranking. Also called inbound links.

Backtest – A retest of a promotion to confirm and give the marketer confidence in the results attained from the original test.

Bait piece – Free content offered to the consumer as an incentive to respond to your email, ad, or other lead-generating promotion. Called a bait piece because it is used as the "bait" in a marketing campaign to hook the prospect, much like a worm dangling from the end of a fishing pole hooks a fish. Also called a lead magnet because of its ability to attract prospects like a magnet attracts metal, and when the prospects click to get the free content, they have opted into your e-list and become a prospect.

What is a Bait Piece?

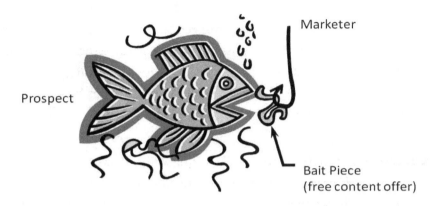

Bait and switch – Offering consumers a product at low cost, and when they click to buy it, they are served a page or sent an email upselling them to a more expensive product.

Bandwidth – (1) How much information (text, images, video, and audio) can be sent through a high-speed digital connection. (2) How much time and attention consumers can or are willing to devote to your marketing messages. (3) The limited amount of time, energy, and patience we as human beings have for tasks, whether reading emails, learning new software, or practicing the violin.

Bangtail – An envelope with an extra flap that is perforated and can be detached; the flap is typically imprinted with an advertising message.

Banner – A rectangular window on a web page with text and graphics for promotional purposes, almost always hyperlinked to a landing page which the visitor can reach by clicking on the banner.

Banner ad – A banner is a small, boxed message that appears atop commercial websites (usually the home page) – or on the first page of an e-zine – and is usually hyperlinked to the advertiser's site.

Bant – An acronym for the four characteristics used to qualify prospects. B is budget: the amount of money the prospect has or is prepared to spend. A is authority: the prospect can authorize and approve the purchase without the permission of a business associate or family member. N is for need: the product has a benefit, feature, or function that the prospect feels is vital for him to obtain. T is for timing: the prospect's need for the product is imminent.

Barcode – A pattern of stripes of varying width that can be read easily by an optical scanner. Barcodes are used on consumer products so the price can be scanned by the cashier in a supermarket checkout line or at a retail store.

Barrier to entry – The degree of difficulty for entering a new market or business. Becoming a plastic surgeon has a high barrier to entry because you need to be a doctor. Starting a carpet cleaning service has a low barrier to entry because you don't need highly specialized training, skills, or equipment.

Basic A ad layout – A standard design for full-page ads in which the top segment of the ad, typically taking up one-third to one-half of the page, is a horizontal photograph or other visual, and the bottom segment contains body copy in two or three columns.

Sidebar (optional)

HEADLINE

VISUAL

HEADLINE

LOGO

800-XXX-XXXX

Basis weight – The weight in pounds of a 500-sheet ream in the basic size for that grade of paper.

BBS (bulletin board system) – Software that enables users to log into email, chat groups, and the **Usenet** via a broadband connection.

BDF (beliefs, desires, feeling) – A formula originated by Mark Ford for writing copy that resonates with the buyer because it reflects her beliefs, desires, and feelings concerning the product and the problem it solves. For instance, many who subscribe to investment newsletters believe big government is bad, feel worried about outliving their retirement savings, and desire greater yield with safety. Experience shows that people who invest in collectible coins tend to be patriotic.

Beauty shot – A photo of a product designed to make the object as visually appealing as possible. For fruit, for example, the photographer sprays the fruit with a fine mist of water before shooting, as water beading up on the skin of the grapes or apples makes them look fresher and more appetizing. For soup, marbles are placed at the bottom of the bowl, so when the soup is ladled on top of the marbles, the soup looks like it is loaded with vegetables and chicken.

Behavior targeting – The ability to segment and reach your audience based on a user's online and offline behavior (i.e., parents shopping for baby goods, connected home users, auto enthusiasts, etc.).

Benefit – What the product does for the buyer, which means how the buyer comes out ahead by using the product. For instance, a benefit of a GPS is you don't need to carry maps or an atlas to navigate your way to your destination.

BETA – Digital business-to-business buyers ages 21 to 41 who hold increasing influence over buying decisions. The letters in the acronym BETA stand for the four key traits of BETAs: blurred boundaries, evolving, tech native, and activist. "Blurred boundaries" means less separation between work and home life. "Evolving" means BETAs use the internet for self-improvement and skills development. "Tech natives" are people who grew up in a world where digital technology always existed, so that smartphones and other tech are an essential part of their life. "Activists" prefer brands and companies that proactively contribute to the good of

Big Data – A mass of data so large that a company's existing computer systems can't properly handle it. The challenge is to find software that can analyze big data in a way the company can use to target prospects more accurately and improve marketing results.

Big idea – A theme for a promotion that is unique and is almost always achieved with "out of the box" thinking. Example: a mailing promoting the stock of an internet infrastructure company that operated a large high-speed backbone network for its customers. Instead of identifying the technology upfront, their marketing campaign euphemistically called it "a new railroad crossing America."

Big ticket – An extremely expensive product representing a major expenditure for a consumer or business buyer. For a consumer, a new car is a big-ticket item. For a plastics company, a new injection molding machine would be a big-ticket item.

Bind-in – A business reply card selling a subscription to a magazine that is bound into an issue of that magazine.

Bill insert – A small piece of paper designed to fit the outer envelope in which a bill is mailed; the insert is imprinted with an advertising message.

Billboard – A large sign, typically 12 by 24 feet, placed by the side of the road to advertise a product, service, or retail location nearby.

Billings – The fees an ad agency charges its clients.

Bill-me – An offer where the prospect can order the product without paying upfront; the customer is invoiced when the product has been delivered. In direct marketing, "bill-me" offers are also called soft offers. While bill-me offers can often generate more gross orders than "cash payment upfront" offers, a significant percentage of bill-me customers typically don't pay the invoice you send them and essentially keep the product without paying you for it.

Binding – The final step in the printing process: gluing, stapling, or stitching the pages of a catalog, brochure, or book to the cover.

Bing – A pay-per-click (PPC) ad network operated by Microsoft in competition with Google Advertising.

Bingo card – Not widely used any more, a **bind-in card** with a series of numbers corresponding to ads in a magazine that have been coded with those numbers. To request sales literature on products, you circle the numbers on the bingo card of the ads featuring products that interest you, then mail back the card to the publisher. The publisher, in turn, passes your inquiry along with those of other readers to the appropriate advertisers. There has long been a belief among some marketers that leads coming in from bingo cards are inferior to leads generated from other response mechanisms, such as phone calls or clicks to a landing page.

Bird's Infallible Alcoholometer (BIA) – A measure of how well you get along with people, a key factor in succeeding in business in general and advertising in particular. The originator of the BIA, ad legend Drayton Bird, said in the ad agency world, one indicator that you got along with people is how often they'd ask you to have drinks with them, hence the reference to "alcohol" in BIA. Lee Iacocca, the former CEO of Chrysler, once said, "If you want to succeed, you'd better get on with people – because that's all we've got around here."

Bit map – Shows the location and color of each pixel on the screen.

Blab – In social media, a platform for live video streaming that allows you to, in essence, have your own small-scale "TV" broadcasts on the internet.

Black hat SEO – The use of questionable and possibly deceptive tactics to raise your site's search engine rankings.

BLAM (Buyer-Lead Account-Based Management) – An empathetic approach, aided by the use of privacy-compliant intent data, to understand exactly what prospective customers are looking for or want to learn more about.

Bleed – An illustration that goes to the edge of the page. Bleed artwork has no borders or margins.

Blind envelope – A plain white direct mail envelope designed to look like personal mail and without teaser copy, company logo, or anything else identifying it as advertising mail.

(A)

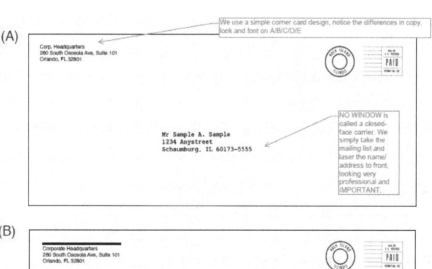

(B)

Blister pack – A product package with a transparent plastic front so the consumer can see the product in its package.

Block – To prevent a consumer from accessing your social media feeds or shopping cart. Example: In my online info product marketing business, we block from our shopping cart customers who have requested three refunds. And a famous social media evangelist threatened to block me from his Facebook wall because I was critical of social media.

Blog – Short for web log. A miniature website where the blogger can write and post short articles, and the blog readers can comment on the articles.

Blog outreach – Contacting bloggers to get them quality guest posts.

Blow in – A business reply card promoting a subscription to a magazine that has been inserted loosely into a copy of that magazine so that it falls out when the magazine is opened.

Blue chip – The stock of highly profitable, publicly-traded, large corporations.

Blueprint – A printer's proof to be checked for errors before a piece is printed; the proof is usually printed in blue ink.

BNLP (buy now, pay later) – When the consumer makes a purchase and takes delivery of the product but is allowed to pay for it in the future, on a specified payment schedule including dates and dollar amounts of installments. Example: You go to a store and buy an expensive couch for $3,000. You sign the paperwork, and the couch is soon delivered to your home. You have promised and are obligated to pay the store $500 a month until you have paid the full $3,000.

BNLP plans either let you get the product with no initial payment, called a *no money down* offer. Or else you make the first payment at the time of purchase and then pay off the balance in installments. The old-fashioned term for BNLP is *lay-away plan.*

Body copy – The main text of an ad or promotion.

Boilerplate – Standard copy used in marketing and product packaging, because of either legal requirements or company policy.

Boldface – Type that is heavier and darker than standard text; **boldface** is often used for headlines and subheads, and sometimes within the body copy to highlight sentences.

BOGO – Stands for buy one, get one free. A popular offer in direct response TV commercials where if you order now, you get another unit of the product free.

Bonus – A gift given free with the purchase of a product.

Book – See *Portfolio.*

Bookalog – A direct mail package that contains a small paperback book, usually sent in an envelope with a cover letter. Covenant House has long used bookalogs for direct mail fundraising. The term "bookalog" refers specifically to the enclosed book. Though the small paperback looks like a regular book, it is, in fact, long sales copy printed in book form.

Booklet – A small, saddle-stitched publication usually providing content as part of a marketing program. Once widely used, printed booklets have been largely replaced today by PDF content as lead magnets.

Bookmark – A web bookmark is an easy way to find your way back to a website – just like a bookmark helps you keep your place in a book you are reading.

Boosted post – A Facebook post that is seen by all of your Facebook friends instead of just some of them because you have paid Facebook a fee to ensure that distribution.

Boot camp – A high-priced, multi-day seminar or training event, usually promoted by entrepreneurs and associations. For a two to four-day boot camp, tuition can range from $1,000 to $5,000 per attendee or more.

Booth – An exhibition at a trade show in which products or information about products are displayed. Many trade show exhibitors line their booth with product images but having actual product samples is usually more effective.

Bounce – This is what happens when email is returned as undeliverable because the address is bad, the domain name is invalid, or the recipient has blocked the sender; it also refers to visitors who leave a website without taking action.

Bounceback – Second mailing sent to a prospective customer who responded to an ad. Bouncebacks are designed to increase response to the initial mailing of product information. Or a catalog, order form, or other insert shipped with a customer's order for the purpose of getting her to place another order.

Bounce rate – The percentage of your emails that bounce back. A high bounce rate means your e-list is dated and needs to be cleaned.

Brace – In typography, a pair of squiggly brackets { }.

Brainstorming – People in a room working to come up with ideas for marketing campaigns, business strategy, new technology, or other creative endeavors.

Brand ambassador – A brand ambassador is a person hired by a company to represent a brand in a positive light, and by doing so, help to increase brand awareness and sales. The methods they use to promote their brand include word-of-mouth marketing; providing feedback and insight on new products and services; responding to inquiries from the public, media, and other organizations; and arranging sponsorship deals.

Brand equity – The goodwill, awareness, memorability, and perception a brand has built up through product quality, service, and marketing.

Brand – The label, name, term, design, or symbol by which a product is identified; the characteristics and personality of a particular product; a product made and marketed under a specific name by a specific company; e.g., Tide laundry detergent.

Brand advertising – Advertising whose primary goal is to promote the brand.

Brand advocate – A customer who is such a big fan of your brand that he goes out of his way to tell other people about it.

Brandcentric – A marketing strategy more concerned with promoting a brand name than generating immediate inquiries and orders.

Branding – A school of advertising that says, "If the consumer has strong recognition and recall of our products, we've done our job." Brand advertising creates product awareness and communicates the brand's attributes or positioning in the marketplace.

Brand essence statement (BES)[3] – A statement reflecting how the consumer perceives the brand, what they think about it, and what they feel about it. The four elements of a BES are: (1) the brand's values and personality, (2) the benefits the brand provides to consumers, both rational and emotional, (3) proof that the brand can deliver on the rational benefits, and (4) a summary statement of what the brand can do for the target consumer.

Brand journalism – When a marketing department operates like a newsroom to research and report on hard-to-find, valuable content that supports the brand.

Brand manager – The person at a company responsible for marketing a particular product or brand.

Break-even point – In direct mail marketing, the number of orders or percentage of responses you have to get so that the net sales generated by the direct mail package are equal to the cost of mailing that package.

Bright shiny object (BSO) – Marketing tactics that are new, hip, or trendy but have not proven themselves to be effective. Some young and inexperienced marketers blindly assume that if a marketing channel or tactic is new, it is automatically better. Experienced marketers use new channels sparingly and test cautiously until the medium has demonstrated its ability to generate positive ROI.

---

3   ANA Business Marketing SmartBrief, 8/27/2021.

Broadband – A data-transmission scheme in which multiple signals share the bandwidth, allowing large files and data-intensive media, such as video, to be transmitted over the internet at high speeds.

Broadside – A one-page promotional flyer folded for mailing. It unfolds into a large flat sheet about the size of a page in a standard newspaper.

Brochure – A print publication, usually with photos or illustrations and quality graphic design, used to promote a product or service. When a prospect inquires about a product, he is often sent an electronic or print brochure.

Brochure collector – A person who loves looking at marketing materials but never buys anything. So named for prospects who go to trade shows and fill plastic bags with sales brochures from practically every booth on the floor, then go home, drop it in a closet, never look at it again, and toss it in the trash when it's time to make more room for clothes in the closet.

Browser – An application used to view information from the internet; e.g., Internet Explorer, Torch, Safari, Mozilla Firefox.

Buck slip – A small insert in a direct mail package, usually measuring 4 by 9 inches. The buck slip can be used for almost anything, but most often, it highlights a premium (see *Premium*) – a free bonus gift given with the order; a guarantee; an option or accessory; an upsell to a deluxe model; or a special product feature. It is called a buck slip because it is roughly the size of a dollar bill.

HEADLINE

#1 _____

#2 _____

#3 _____

〜〜〜〜〜〜 **800-XXX-XXXX**

Budget – The amount of money the advertiser plans to spend on advertising.

Bulk mailing – The mailing of a large number of identical pieces of third-class mail at a reduced rate.

Bullets – Heavy dots used to separate lines or paragraphs of copy.

- First bullet.

- Second bullet.

- Third bullet.

Bundling – Grouping multiple products and offering them as a package at a discounted price.

Buried ad – An ad surrounded by other ads. Much more desirable is to have an ad surrounded by articles, which get greater readership than ads. Buried ads tend to get lost, and their response is reduced as a result.

Buried offer – An offer made in the body copy of a promotion rather than in the headline and the close.

Burst – A graphic that looks somewhat like an exploding star to call attention to text within the burst; this text is typically a call-to-action hyperlinked to a web page. Or it might be a short bit of copy; e.g., "Valentine's Day Sale – 25% Off!"

Business case – Arguments and proof that a marketing tactic or campaign is likely to generate a positive return on investment. Managers may require marketers to make a business case for a proposed campaign before giving the go-ahead. It can also apply to any business decision or action; e.g., purchase of a forklift, new sprinklers for your plant.

Business Marketing Association – A trade association catering to business-to-business marketers.

Business opportunity – A course, program, or other offering to train the buyer or otherwise help her get started in a specific small business, usually home-based. For instance, *Locksmithing School*[4] sells training in locksmithing to laypeople as a new career or business opportunity.

Business reply card (BRC) – A reply card addressed to the marketer with a business reply permit code, which allows the prospect to mail back the reply card to the marketer without paying postage; postage is paid by the marketer. Used primarily in direct mail packages that generate leads.

---

4   https://locksmithingschool.com/about/

Business reply envelope (BRE) – A reply envelope addressed to the marketer with a business reply permit code, which allows the prospect to mail back the envelope to the marketer without paying postage; postage is paid by the marketer. Used primarily in direct mail packages that either are asking for an order or confidential information the prospect would not like his mail carrier or anyone else to see.

Business reply permit – A permit from the post office you can use to print business reply cards or envelopes that prospects can mail back to you, the marketer, without affixing postage. You pay the postage, but only on the cards and envelopes actually returned to you, not on all the cards and envelopes printed. This is why using a business reply permit makes a lot more sense than affixing postage stamps to all your reply cards and envelopes; if you do that, you are paying postage whether the card or envelope is mailed back to you or not. Crazy and a waste of money.

Business-to-business (B2B) advertising – Advertising of products and services sold by a business to other businesses.

Business-to-consumer (B2C) advertising – Advertising of products and services sold to consumers.

Business-to-government (B2G) advertising – Advertising of products and services sold to federal, state, and local governments.

Buttons – Graphics on your screen that serve as 2D click buttons. On your website, these buttons direct users to specific pages; e.g., product pages. Buttons are also used in emails and online ads, where they most often take the user to a website or other web page. On landing pages, users click **Order Now** buttons to order a product or other buttons to download free content or submit online forms.

Which Order Button Pulled Best?

- o Test A - **Order Now!** (white text on red)
- o Test B - **Order Now!** (white text on green)
- o Test C - Order Now! (black text on yellow)
- o Test D - Order Now! (deep blue text on ochre)

Button ad – Small banner ads measuring 125 by 125 pixels or smaller; often placed in the margins of the screen.

Buyer's club – Customers are treated as members of a club and, as such, get periodic special offers and other privileges. Airlines, for instance, have special lounges in airports that can be used only by their elite members.

Buying influence – Any person who influences the purchase decision; e.g., the CEO, CFO, purchasing agent, plant engineer, IT manager. In business-to-business marketing, the four major categories of buying influences are executive (e.g., CEO), financial (e.g., CFO), technical (e.g., IT manager), and end-user (managers and other staff).

Buying the business – Selling your product at a price so low as to be unprofitable; done to entice people to buy and thereby become your customer. The problem with buying the business is that it spoils the prospects into expecting these low prices to continue, making it difficult to make a decent profit selling more products to them. Also known as a loss leader.

C

Canonical – An HTML element added into the head of a webpage that webmasters use to prevent duplicate content issues. The code RFC 6596 is added to the HTML code to alert Google crawlers of duplicate page content. Only the original or "canonical" version of the web page content is specified as part of search engine optimization credit to the webmaster. Duplicate content on the web should point to the canonical source URL, providing SEO credit solely to the web page with the original content.

Cache – A storage area for frequently accessed information.

Caging – Opening envelopes with orders and checks and counting the money in a secure environment, typically a caged room is monitored by video cameras to prevent theft of cash orders.

Call to action (CTA) – The part of the promotion that tells the prospect what action to take. On a website, a CTA is typically a button that, when clicked, goes to a form the prospect can fill out and submit to get something – a newsletter, a report, a product – in return.

Call center – A facility equipped and staffed to handle outbound and inbound telemarketing calls.

Call-out – A short block of copy describing a product feature or benefit, with a line connecting the copy block to approximately where the feature may be found in a photo of the product.

Camera-ready – Finished artwork and page layouts that are ready to be printed.

Campaign – A coordinated program of advertising and promotion.

Comment spam – When people leave nonsense or irrelevant comments in response to a blog post for the purpose of getting a link to the spammer's website on the blog.

CAN-SPAM – Laws prohibiting spamming.

CASL – Canada's anti-spam legislation; their version of CAN-SPAM.

Captcha – A small box on a landing page or web form that asks you to type in the characters you see in an image.

Caption – Text explaining a photo or illustration, usually printed in italics under the visual. Many marketers do not use captions, but research has shown that they, in fact, get higher readership than the body copy.

Card deck – A group of promotional postcards, each from a different advertiser, mailed together in a shrink wrap; each advertiser pays to have their card in the deck.

Card mailer – A direct mail package that contains a faux membership or credit card as an attention-getting device.

Case study – A marketing document showing how a customer solved their problem using your product.

Catalog – A bound publication advertising multiple products with photos and descriptions and usually prices.

CGI (common gateway interface) – An interface-creation scripting program that allows web pages to be made on the fly based on information from buttons, checkboxes, text input, and so on.

CHAID (chi-squared automatic interactive detector) – A marketing model that estimates the probability that one variable is dependent on another variable; e.g., that being Jewish correlated to buying hot dogs.

Character – An animated or live fictional spokesperson for the company; e.g., Sam Breakstone, Captain Crunch, the Jolly Green Giant.

Chat room – An area online where you can chat with other members in real-time.

Celebrity endorsement – Advertising in which a celebrity is paid to say he uses, likes, and recommends the marketer's product.

Cell size – The number of names in a cell being tested in a direct mail or email marketing program. The standard wisdom is that each test cell must have 5,000 names for the test to be statistically valid. Other mailers have found that 2,000 names per test cell generate valid test results.

CHAD – Change of address.

Channel – A method of communicating with consumers. e.g., magazine ads are one channel, TV commercials are another.

Character count – The number of characters that can fit a given space or are allowed to be used in an online ad.

Chatbot – An icon, image, button, or other device on a company's website that users can click to communicate with the company. Some chat bots bring up a window where you can interactively communicate by typing statements, questions, and responses. Others enable you to connect with a salesperson via a phone or online call. Some chat bots put you with a live person on the other end who is doing the talking, while others are driven by AI software to give automated responses with no live salesperson or customer service representative on the other side. The American Writers and Artists Inc. has coined the term **"nano-writing"** to describe copywriting for chat bots.

Cheesecake – The use of attractive, scantily clad models in a commercial, ad, or trade show exhibit to gain people's attention. In trade shows, also known as booth babes.

Cheshire label – A type of mailing label affixed to direct mail envelopes and reply elements.

Churn – The rate at which a business loses customers.

Circles – User-defined groups of friends on Google+ to which the user can post messages to exclusively if he so wishes.

Circulars – Inserts delivered with the Sunday newspaper, usually in color and printed on thin stock, most often for retail offers or local service businesses.

Circulation – The number of people who read or receive a publication, such as a newspaper or trade journal.

Classified ad – A small, all-text ad that runs in a special classified ad section in the back of a newspaper or magazine. You pay based on the number of words in the ad.

Classified display ad – A small display ad that has design and possibly images but runs in the classified ad section; usually no more than one or two inches deep.

Click – The opportunity for a visitor to be transferred to a location on a website or the internet by clicking on a hyperlink.

Clickbait – Web content or online advertising with a misleading or sensationalist headline that entices people to click through to a web page, usually with the goal of generating page views, list opt-ins, or product sales.

Click Bank – An online marketplace for digital information products. It aims to serve as a connection between digital content creators who publish the information products and affiliate marketers who promote and sell these digital information products to consumers.

Click button – A button you click online that takes you to a specific web page via a hyperlink.

Click-to-open rate (CTOR) – A calculation that tracks the percentage of click-throughs of those emails that were actually opened. CTOR can provide additional insight on the effectiveness of the email.

Click-to-purchase rate – The number of purchases generated by an email campaign divided by the number of emails opened.

Click-stream – A click-stream is a record of what a user clicks on while web browsing. As the user clicks anywhere in the website, the action is logged on a client or inside the web server.

Click-through rate (CTR) – The percentage of users viewing an online ad or email who click on a hyperlink to reach the web page to which the link is attached. One of the keys to generating more leads and orders online is to improve the CTR; the other is to boost website and landing page conversion rates.

Client – (1) A company that uses the services of advertising professionals. (2) A computer connected to a server.

Clio – Advertising-industry award given for the best television commercials of the year.

Clipping service – A company that monitors the media for mentions or stories about you or your company and sends them to you.

Closed-loop marketing – Sales reports on the quality and status of leads provided to them by marketing, providing another means of measuring lead quality by source, promotion, or offer.

Closing date – The date by which the finished ad or commercial must be at the publication or station to appear in a specific issue or time slot.

Close-out – Unsold inventory, usually of products no longer in fashion, style, or demand, or that have been made obsolete by this year's model. The manufacturer or wholesaler offers the merchandise for volume purchase – to recover part of the cost of the inventory and also to free up valuable warehouse space. These close-out products are usually bought and then resold by stores or dealers who specialize in close-out sales.

Closed ecosystem (Walled Garden) – Content that requires a subscription or is behind a paywall, meaning you have to sign up to listen.

Cluster analysis – Analyzing your customer data and determining which zip codes have the greatest chance of success for your mailings; grouping variables based on similar data characteristics to segment customers based on demographics, psychographic, and purchase behavior.

Clustering – Grouping individual records on a list or database according to geographic, psychographic, or demographic characteristics; e.g., every household in a town living in a home costing a million dollars or more.

CMYK color – In printing, creating a four-color document by mixing four basic ink colors: cyan, magenta, yellow, and black; these are known as process colors because they are used in a four-color printing process.

Coated paper stock – Papers coated with pigments, binders, and other materials to improve surface gloss. Most consumer magazines are printed on coated stock.

COD (Cash on Delivery) – The U.S. Postal Service or United Parcel service delivers the product you ordered and collects the payment from you.

Cohort analysis – A marketing analytic that identifies relationships between characteristics of a population or group of people and that population's behavior. For a publisher of an annual directory, cohort analysis shows that of those who purchase an annual directory, the buyers who purchased three years ago were the most likely to buy this year's edition.

Cold calling – Approaching prospects by phone call or door-to-door visits without having had any prior contact with them.

Cold lists – Mailing lists for which the people on the list have no relationship with the marketer.

Collaborative filtering – An algorithm that makes recommendations to consumers based on the actions of other consumers on the site. For instance, if the algorithm found that a lot of customers who bought A also bought Y, then when you buy A, the algorithm will suggest that you might also like Y.

Collate – (1) To assemble individual elements of a mailing in sequence for inserting into a direct mail envelope; usually done by a letter shop. (2) To assemble loose sheets into a booklet, catalog, or brochure during the binding process.

Collateral – Printed product information such as brochures, flyers, catalogs, datasheets, and direct mail.

Color separation – Full-color printing achieved using four separate printing plates for cyan, magenta, yellow, and black.

Column-inch – The measure of the size of a newspaper ad. An ad that is two columns wide and three inches deep is six column inches.

Comment – A response to a blog or Facebook post that appears online.

Commission – In internet marketing, a fee paid to the organization or individual who drove traffic to your landing page, resulting in a sale. Commissions range from 10 percent to 50 percent of gross revenues; there is no commission paid on shipping and handling charges.

Commodity product – A product that is pretty much the same as all other products in its category, with little or nothing to distinguish it.

Comp, comprehensive – A drawing of the proposed layout for an ad or other promotion. When the comp is approved, then the actual ad is put into layout by the graphic designer.

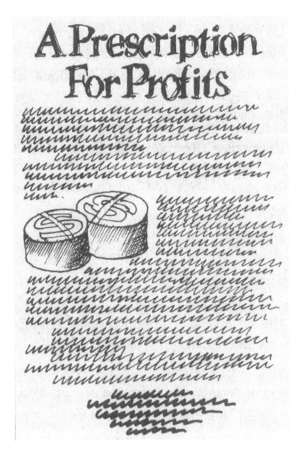

Comparative advertising – Advertising that claims your product is superior to another product and identifies that product by its brand name.

Competitive content marketing analysis – A process of reviewing competitors' content to ensure your content is different and more compelling.

Compiled list – A mailing list compiled from some data source such as municipal records, phone directories, association membership directories, newspapers, trade journals, trade show attendees, and websites. Example: a list of homeowners compiled from municipal records. There is no evidence that the individuals on any given compiled list have ever responded to a direct marketing solicitation before, so whether they will respond to any is uncertain.

Compliance – Making sure marketing copy follows all the laws, rules, and regulations for a product category or marketing channel. For instance, copy promoting a dietary supplement cannot claim that the pill cures any disease. An ad for a prostate supplement cannot say it is used to treat benign prostate hyperplasia (BPH); it can say it promotes optimal prostate health.

Computer to plate – Data from the computer is imaged directly onto a printing plate, which is a foil, without using film as an intermediary.

Concentration – Focusing your marketing on the prospects most likely to buy while bypassing those who are unlikely to buy.

Concept – The overriding logic and creative approach to an ad or marketing campaign.

Concertina fold – Continuous parallel folding of brochures in the manner of an accordion, where the fold is alternatively made to the front and back; also called accordion fold.

Connected packaging – Product packaging with a QR code the customer can scan with a smartphone to access more detailed product information than is printed on the box. According to research from SharpEnd, consumers see the most value in connected packaging tie-ins for luxury and nonluxury clothing and footwear.

Connected TV (CTV) – Use of a smart TV, gaming console, or other internet-connected device to watch TV and video content online.

Considered purchase – A purchase made after careful evaluation of the product.

Consultative selling – A sales and marketing approach where the marketer hopes to make a sale by serving the role of unpaid consultant and solving the customer's problem. The solution, of course, required purchase of the salesperson's product.

Consumer advertising – Advertising of products sold to the general public.

Consumer packaged goods – Products that are consumable (e.g., shampoo, canned soup), wear out (e.g., sneakers, underwear), or have a limited operating life and then stop working (e.g., light bulbs, burner cell phones) and therefore must be replenished or replaced. Packaged goods are sold to consumers through both retail and e-commerce.

Consumer products – Goods sold to individuals rather than to business or industry.

Consumer – One who buys or uses products and services.

Content – Useful or interesting information given to consumers as part of the marketing effort. For instance, you might give a homeowner a booklet on how to avoid contractor rip-offs if you are a contractor selling your own services. Popular types of content include videos, blog posts, white papers, articles, and podcasts.

Content, long-form – Content that is 1,000 words or longer.[5] Examples of long-form content include how-to articles, white papers, and case studies. Casual visitors don't often read long copy – but who cares? Serious prospects read long-form copy to dig deeper into applications, products, and technologies. Also, pages with long-form content often achieve higher search engine rankings.

Content, strategic – Content tailored to a specific audience to achieve a specific objective; e.g., to move the prospect to take the next step in the buying process; educate the prospects on your technology or application; build greater awareness of your brand or value proposition.

Content curation – The process of sifting through the web to find the best and most relevant content for an audience and then presenting it to them either as-is or augmented by you with editing or editorial comments. Content curation is not creating new content. It is creating value for your audience by bringing to their attention content of interest or use to them.

Content marketing – Marketing campaigns that focus on the creation and distribution of content to persuade the consumer to trust your company, convince him that you are an expert and reliable source, and ultimately to get him to buy your product.

---

5   GlobalSpec Marketing Maven, 8/5/2021.

Content management system (CMS) – Software that enables website owners and users to change or add content to the website without programming or help from IT.

Content syndication – Pushing your blog, articles, and other content onto third-party sites, either as a full post, an abstract, or a link to the content on your site. The idea is to distribute your content to a broader audience. The benefits are more traffic for your own site or more exposure for your brand – or for you.

Content tags – HTML labels that define the essence of the content contained in a web page. The content tags are readable by spiders, allowing search engines to find the pages and rank them. Also called meta tags.

Contest – Sales promotion in which the consumer uses his skill to try and win a prize. Some contests require proof of purchase.

Contextual targeting – A machine scans page content. Contextual targeting software (e.g., DoubleVerify, Integral Ad Science, Oracle Contextual Intelligence) uses natural language processing to understand the meaning and nuances of articles. Ads most closely related to the article are served to users viewing that content on their screen.[6]

Continuity program – An offer where the customer agrees to buy a series of products on a recurring basis, such as the Beer of the Month Club or the state quarters coin collection.

Control – A marketer's best-performing direct mail package. Serious direct mail marketers are constantly creating and testing new mailings

---

6   https://www.adexchanger.com/online-advertising/the-crawl-walk-run-guide-to-contextual-targeting/

in an effort to beat or outpull the control mailing, which has until this point beaten all other mailers promoting the product. The term control today is applied to many other marketing channels in addition to direct mail. The performance of new promotions being tested in that channel is measured against the control. When a test beats the current control, it becomes the new control.

Controlled circulation – A trade journal or magazine given away free to people who qualify, usually by virtue of being in a particular profession or industry.

Conversational commerce – The use of chatbots, apps, call centers, and other technology to enable consumers to communicate with brands, merchants, and service providers in a more direct, conversational, and personal manner; e.g., the user clicks a chatbot icon on the website home page and is immediately connected to a live or AI customer service rep. Conversational commerce enables customers to ask questions, make requests, or provide feedback at any point in the buying process.

Conversion – Getting an online user to take a specific action, typically registering online in exchange for free content or purchasing a product from a website. The conversion rate is the percentage of prospects exposed to a marketing tactic who take the action encouraged by the marketing. For instance, if you drive 100 people to a landing page where you are offering a free white paper, and 14 complete your registration form and download the PDF, your conversion rate is 14 percent.

Conversion effort – An email or letter designed to turn a lead or inquiry into a purchase.

Conversion path – The steps a prospect goes through to become either a lead, a qualified prospect, or a customer. (See also *Sales Funnel.*)

Conversion rate – The percentage of people who start and complete your call to action.

Conversion series – A timed and coordinated series of efforts. The number of efforts in the series can range from two to dozens, but seven efforts is a common number.

Cookie – A file on your computer that records information such as where you have been on the web. The browser stores this information, which allows a site to remember where it has been in future transactions or requests.

Cookie buster – Software that blocks the placement of cookies on a user's browser.

Co-op – When a manufacturer and a retailer selling the manufacturer's product split the cost of an ad promoting sale of the product at the retailer's store. The term *co-op budget* refers to the amount of money a manufacturer has set aside to help fund ad campaigns by their retailers, distributors, and others selling the product.

Coopetition – When businesses that are normally competitors cooperate or collaborate with each other for mutual benefit; e.g., people who sell info products on marketing are my competitors, but if I like their products, I will often sell them my list for an affiliate commission.

Copy – The text of an ad, commercial, or promotion.

Copy amplifier – A "copy amplifier" is a brief sentence or phrase added to follow a line of copy to make it more impactful. For instance, instead of "This offer expires December 31, 2022," write "This offer expires December 31, 2022. After that, it's too late." Instead of "Only so many copies will be printed," write "Only so many copies will be printed. No more."

Copy brief – A document prepared to guide the copywriter in his preparation of the copy. The brief typically contains a description of the product and its features and benefits, positioning of the product in the marketplace, and detailed information on the target market.

Copycat – An ad so similar to another ad that it borders on plagiarism.

Copy/Contact – An ad agency copywriter who works directly with the client instead of through an account executive.

Copy cub – A beginning copywriter, usually being trained by a senior copywriter.

Copywriter – A person who writes copy.

Core buying complex – Refers to the consumer's psychological make-up as it influences her purchase of your product. The core buying complex has three elements: (1) beliefs – what the consumer thinks, (2) desires – what the consumer wants, and (3) feelings – the emotions the consumer feels in connection with your product. For instance, in the core buying complex used for marketing collectible coins, coin collectors are known to have higher-than-average feelings of patriotism and distrust of big government.

Core dump – Giving your copywriter or agency a massive amount of information to help them create the best promotion possible. It is better for the creative team to get too much information rather than too little.

Co-registration – You land on a squeeze page to accept an offer. On the page, there is a line that says something like, "You may be interested in these related offers." Underneath are half a dozen offers for other products. You can click to select the ones you are interested in, and those marketers get your opt-in when you submit the page to get the primary offer. Those half a dozen other marketers have paid an advertising charge to be on that page. This is a co-registration: you register for the other offers in addition to the primary offer.

Corner card – The upper left corner of the front of an envelope. The mailer's return address is usually printed either on the corner card or on the rear flap.

Corporate advertising – Ads that promote a corporation to bolster its image.

Corporate identity – A system of graphics – everything from logo and letterhead to envelopes and guidelines for ad design – that are the standard to which a company's materials must be designed.

Cost per click – The amount of money advertisers pay Google, Bing, or other advertising media for each click on the advertiser's ad.

Cost per inquiry – Divide the total cost of the marketing campaign by the total number of inquiries received to calculate the cost paid to generate each inquiry. The costs used in the calculation are usually the recurring costs; e.g., the media cost to air a radio commercial, and not the one-time creative cost to write and design the promotion.

Cost per name – The marketing cost of adding a new name or subscriber to your opt-in e-list.

Cost per thousand (CPM) – The cost to buy a thousand of anything related to marketing; e.g., mailing lists, postage for direct mail packages.

Country code top level domain (CCTLD) – Domain suffix showing what country a site is from; e.g., .com.au is the CCTDL for Australia.

Coupon – A certificate redeemable for a product discount or free bonus gift, or a form in an ad you can fill out and return to the advertiser to get more information or place an order.

Co-viewing – Sharing content with others on Twitter; an article in ANA Business Marketing Smart Brief (1/21/20) reports that 44 percent of people using the leading social media platform said their usage of Twitter while watching TV increased in 2020 – with social distancing being one of the reasons.

CPA – Cost per acquisition: Paying for advertising per response. That response could be a lead, a sale, a registration, an opt-in, or whatever the advertiser and owner of the ad network agree upon.

CPC – Cost per click: how much money an advertiser pays for each click generated by his ad. Usually applies to pay-per-click ads on Google and Bing.

CPL – Cost per lead. Amount of money spent in marketing to generate a lead.

CPM – The price to rent a list per 1,000 names mailed. Or the cost you pay for online advertising for every 1,000 impressions your ad receives.

CPO – Cost per order. Amount of money spent in marketing to generate an order.

CPP – Cost per thousand prospects.

Crawler – A search engine algorithm that scours the web in search of web pages, which it stores in the search engine's index. These pages are displayed when search engine users do a keyword search for keywords contained in the page's text or metatags. Also called spiders or robots.

Creator economy – A distribution model for creative content creation under which individuals can, often profitably, publish their content on their own without either the help or control of the media and other centralized corporations. Creators disseminate their content largely through social media platforms such as TikTok and YouTube.

Creative – A copywriter, graphic artist, photographer, or anyone else who handles the creative part of making a promotion.

Crits (criticisms) – Revisions to ad copy requested by the client.

Cross-channel attribution – Determining which of your marketing channels are most responsible for sales.

Cross-sell – When the consumer buys product A, offering him product B at the time of purchase. The products are not in the same category but are often related; e.g., you buy a fly fishing rod, and the salesperson suggests you also buy wading boots for standing in the stream.

CRP – Cost per response. The cost to get a response to your marketing campaign. Calculated by taking the total cost of the promotion and dividing by the number of responses received.

CPT – Cost per transaction. Amount of money spent in marketing to generate a specific action such as a download or sale.

CPTM – Cost per targeted thousand impressions. Amount of money spent to generate 1,000 impressions.

Creative director – Ad-agency employee responsible for supervising the work of copywriters, art directors, and others who produce advertising.

Creative – Describes activities directly related to the creation of advertising. These include copywriting, photography, illustration, and design.

Creative Commons – A nonprofit corporation that makes it easier for people to create new content based upon the work of others while adhering to the rules of copyright.

Cross-promotion – When two companies, often owned by the same conglomerate, help sell each other's products to each other's prospects and customers.

Cross-screen – Marketing campaigns that reach consumers on multiple screens, devices, and formats including linear TV, OTT, CTV, social media, and others.

Crush it – Refers to the performance of a marketing campaign that is generating results beyond all expectations and making a lot of money for the marketer.

CSS (cascading style sheet) – A method of moving style elements of web pages to allow for faster loading and smaller file sizes. The CSS is code that determines how your website's HTML displays on the screen.

CRM (customer relationship management) – Software that helps companies provide superior service and a better user experience to their customers. For instance, the CRM can show the sales department all the prospects who have not been visited by a sales rep within the last 12 months.

Cumulative audience – The number of unduplicated people or households watching a commercial or seeing an ad.

Curate – To take content from other sources and publish it on your site or in your e-newsletter, giving credit to the original author. By curating content, you bring your audience useful and interesting information they might not otherwise see.

Customer acquisition cost – The amount of money you spend in marketing to get a stranger to make their first purchase from you and thereby become a customer. If you run a newspaper ad for $5,000 and fifty people call and order the product, your customer acquisition cost is $100.

Customer data platform (CDP) – A database that contains complete information on customers, often gathered by the database software from multiple IT sources; e.g., accounting software, CRM, analytics.

Customer journey maps – All the steps a customer must take to purchase from a retailer and how they feel at each of those steps.

Customer persona – A detailed written description of who a company's ideal customer would be, including the customers' demographics and psychographics.

Customer relationship management (CRM) – A software system that helps manage the company's ongoing relationship with each customer. Includes customer service, retention, and cross-selling.

Customer experience (CX) – While UX refers mainly to the user's experience with your website, CX refers to practically everything that the customer experiences when dealing with your company – from how you answer the phone or respond to email queries, to how you handle product returns and field service repairs, to whether you are on time for appointments or with product delivery dates.

D

Daily flash report – A report showing the number of inquiries received per day while a promotion is running.

Dance card – The list of potential clients wanting to hire a particular vendor but having to wait until the vendor has time in his schedule.

Database – A collection of consumer or business records searchable by fields. More broadly, any organized assemblage of related data. The data on a particular customer is called a *record*. The individual data points in that record – customer name, date of last purchase, job title – are called *fields* or variables.

Database marketing – Marketing campaigns designed around creative or strategic use of a marketer's database. For instance, if a marketing database has fields in all records for the last time the customers attending a seminar or other event sponsored by the advertiser, they could do a campaign offering a special discount for attendees of the events only.

Data card – A sales sheet promoting a mailing list available for rental by direct mailers.

Data mining – Applying statistical analysis to large volumes of data for discovering consumer behavioral patterns and buying habits.

Data service bureau – Business with powerful computers capable of manipulating and analyzing large volumes of data in a short period of time.

Datasheet – A sales sheet printed on one or both sides of an 8 1/2 by 11-inch sheet of paper or PDF, presenting features and specifications of a product. The front usually describes the product and its features and benefits, while the reverse side presents the specifications.

Data suppression – eliminating unwanted records from the names in a list you select for your marketing campaigns. For instance, some merchants suppress the names of "serial returners" – customers who repeatedly buy products that they quickly return after using them once, such as a pair of expensive shoes "borrowed" in this questionable matter for a wedding or other special occasion. There are many other people you may want to remove from the list, including competitors, prisoners, and difficult customers.

Day part – The time of day a TV or radio commercial is aired.

Deadline – A date by which the consumer must respond to the promotion to take advantage of the offer.

Decision-maker – The person who makes the buying decision; e.g., in a household where the family is considering getting a dog, the decision-makers are the parents, not the children.

Dedicated email – An email dedicated to promoting a single product.

De-dupe – To remove duplicate names from a database or collection of mailing lists.

Demand generation – Marketing programs implemented with the goal of increasing consumer desire and demand for a product or service. Demand generation campaigns are usually data-driven and multichannel.

Demassification – The transformation of the mass market into multiple niche markets.

Demographic overlay – Adding demographic data to a prospect or customer list by running it through the computer and matching it against other lists that already contain the data.

Demographics – Statistics describing the characteristics of a segment of the population. These characteristics include age, sex, income, marital status, presence of children in household, home ownership, net worth, religion, and race.

Demonstration – A TV commercial, online video, or other marketing that sells the product by demonstrating how it works; e.g., commercial selling juicers.

Description tag – A meta tag that describes you and your offerings. This tag is the descriptive text that appears when your company is found and displayed on the search engine results page.

Die cut – In the printing process, using a die to cut a shape out of a piece of stiff paper for decorative purposes. When done in a brochure or greeting card, the reader can see through the portions that have been cut away to whatever is printed on the next page, which is a consideration in the design.

Differentiation – A feature or other attribute that makes your product different than all other products in its category.

Digest – A saddle-stitched booklet used as a self-mailer, with the page size 3 ½ inches wide by 10 inches high.

Digg – A social news website that allows members to submit articles and vote for the ones they want to appear on the home page of the site.

Digital dirt – Negative comments about you, your product, or your company posted online.

Digital marketing – Marketing products and services online.

Digital printing – Printing processes in which the information is transferred from the computer to the paper without the intermediaries of plates or film. You get better quality with plates or film, but digital printing is faster and cheaper for short runs.

Direct mail – Unsolicited advertising material delivered by mail.

Direct mail co-op packages – Envelopes filled with advertisements from multiple marketers. Each marketer pays the co-op producer a fee to include their ad in the envelope.

Direct mail package – Advertising matter mailed unsolicited in an envelope. Elements can include an outer envelope, sales letter, reply card or order form, business reply envelope, buck slip, brochure, lift note, and any other additional inserts.

Direct response – Advertising that seeks to get orders or leads directly and immediately rather than build an image or awareness over a period of time; also called direct marketing or direct response marketing.

Direct response TV (DRTV) – Television commercials that sell products to the viewers directly by getting them to call a toll-free number or, in some cases, buy online at a specific website URL. Short-term direct response commercials are usually 2 minutes long. (See also *Infomercials*.)

Directory – A paperback volume or website page of compiled information in alphabetical order; e.g., the membership directory of your town's Chamber of Commerce.

Discovery process – The steps a copywriter takes to find out enough about the product and the target market to write strong advertising for that product.

Discovery shopping – When retailers deliberately move different products or entire sections to different aisles, forcing consumers to wander the store searching for what they want to buy, and in the process, making them encounter other goods they might need.

Display advertising – All ads in print publications other than classified.

Disruptive – An innovative technology or product that changes the way marketing is done. Examples include the internet and smartphones.

Domain name – The unique web address for your site. Mine is www. bly.com.

Domain part of the DNS (domain naming system) – Name that specifies details about the host. A domain is the main subdivision of internet addresses, the last three letters after the final dot, and it tells you what kind of organization you are dealing with. There are six top-level domains widely used in the U.S.: .com (commercial), .edu (educational), .net (network operations), .gov (U.S. government), .mil (U.S. military), and .org (organization).

Dominant resident emotion – This is the primary emotion the prospect has in relation to your product or the problem it solves. For example, the publisher of an options trading software package, understanding that the dominant resident emotion concerning options trading products is skepticism, tripled sales with this headline: "Why your options trading software doesn't work . . . and never will."

Donor list – A list of people who have contributed to worthy causes, used in fundraising direct mail campaigns.

Do Not Call List – A database of consumers who do not want to receive telemarketing calls; telemarketers face substantial fines for phoning people who are on the do not call list.

Door-to-door (D2D) – A form of face-to-face cold calling type, D2D selling is done by sales reps who walk through a neighborhood and knock on doors in the hopes they can sell a product to the homeowner or tenant. If the salesperson does not have a license, it is considered **peddling.**

Door hanger – A small advertising card the marketer hangs on the doors of people in a neighborhood that represents his target market.

Doorway – A domain or page created to rank high in the search engines for specific keywords. When the user searches the keyword, the domain and page come up. When the users click the domain page URL, they are redirected to the marketer's main domain and website home page.

Dot gain – The growth in the size of screen dots during the prepress and press stages; when dots become too large, it can cause color shifts in the printed piece.

Double-truck – A two-page spread in a print publication where the ad runs across the middle gutter.

Double opt in – You sign up to opt into someone's e-list. Before you are added to the list, you get an email asking you to confirm that in fact you do want to opt into the list. That's called a double opt in since you essentially are asked to opt in twice.

Doubling day – The day when half the orders a direct mail package is going to produce have been received. If you know when doubling day is based on experience – say, 14 days after the mailing drops – then when you reach doubling day, you multiply the number of orders received so far by 2 to forecast the total response to the mailing.

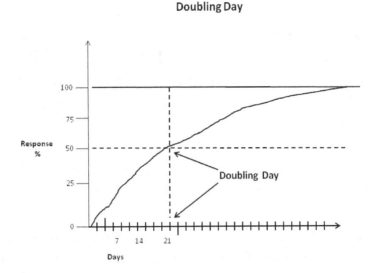

Doubling Day

Douchefluence – A marketing strategy of offending and alienating non-core audiences and opposing forces in order to position yourself more strongly with your target audience. It forges an emotional connection with your target audience, many of whom had contempt for the other audiences you are disparaging. Often used in generational marketing.

Downscale – Consumers on the low end of the social scale in terms of income, education, and status.

Drill down – A term used to express what a surfer does as he or she goes further into a website, clicking on secondary and tertiary pages.

Drive time – Radio commercials airing during morning and evening rush hour, drive time spots are the most expensive because more people are listening as they commute.

Drops – An Instagram feature that serves users content on new products and offers related to each user's interests.

Drop shadow – A shadow behind large letters in a headline or poster that give the lettering almost a 3D effect.

Dummy – A mock-up of a marketing brochure, direct mail package, or other marketing piece created for approval by the client before proceeding with final artwork and printing.

Dupe – In a direct mail campaign where the mailer is being sent to multiple mailing lists, a dupe is a name that appears on more than one list.

Drip campaign – A series of mailings or emails to generate as many leads and sales as possible from a given group of prospects.

Drop – To take your direct mail packages to the post office and mail them. The date on which you do this is the drop date.

Drop-down menu – When you click a field on an online form, a list of items to choose from – e.g., state, country, age, number of employees in your firm – drops down and allows you to select one.

Dry testing – Testing a promotion before the product is ready to be sold and shipped. If the test works, the marketer makes or acquires the product and fills orders. If the test fails, the marketer notifies the consumers and returns any payments received.

Dwell rate – The percentage of users exposed to a given piece of rich media content or online advertising who interact with that content by moving their cursors over it but do not click on it.

Dwell time – The amount of time the user spends on a page before leaving to take another action.

Dying industry – Any industry or trade that was at one time active, thriving, and in demand but is declining so that the industry is becoming either obsolete or ending altogether. For example, coal mining is in decline because of the switch away from fossil fuels to renewable energy sources. Photography as a trade is in decline because smartphones make it easy for non-photographers to take good pictures.

Dynamic content – Different content is delivered to different users based on past activity or other data possessed by your system.

Dynamic rotation – Serving the user a series of different banner ads randomly on a rotating basis. Users see different ads on different pages of the website.

E

Earned media – Media exposure that you don't have to pay for; e.g., free publicity.

Early adopter – A consumer who likes to be among the first to buy a new type of product, especially technology products like notebooks and smartphones.

Early bird discount – A discount on a product or service offered to people who buy it now rather than later; also refers to a discount on an event for early registration.

Early bird renewal – A notice to renew a subscription sent six months or more before the subscription is due to expire.

Earnings per click (EPC) – Revenue produced by online marketing per hundred clicks.

E-book – A digital book that is either a downloadable PDF or sold in Kindle format on Amazon.

E-commerce – Using electronic information technologies on the internet to allow direct selling and automatic processing of purchases between parties.

Editorial calendar – A magazine's schedule of special issues and feature articles, typically by main topic, planned for a full year of publication. For instance, if a monthly trade magazine plans a special section on biohazard containment for its November issue, sending them a press release or article query on biohazards in advance of that can increase your chances of getting featured in that publication.

E-list – A list of people and their email addresses.

Email – An abbreviation for electronic mail, which is a network service that allows users to send and receive messages via computer.

Email blast – Distributing an email to a large number of recipients all at once.

E-newsletter – An electronic newsletter delivered via email.

401 Error – An error message users receive when they attempt to go to a web page that does not exist.

E-zine – A part-promotional, part-informational newsletter or magazine distributed on the internet. Also called an e-newsletter.

Editorial – Those portions of a magazine's or newspaper's reading matter that are not advertisements – articles, news briefs, fillers, and other material produced by the publication's editors and writers.

Educainment – A promotion that entertains as it educates.

Elevator pitch – A prewritten and rehearsed short answer you give when someone you meet asks you, "What do you do?"

Email marketing – Mass distribution of an email containing a sales message to multiple recipients, all on one or more e-lists.

Embossing – A printing process in which a pattern is raised on the surface of paper. The raised pattern is part of the paper itself, as opposed to engraving, in which the raised pattern is made by applying ink to the paper.

Emoticons – The online means of facial expression and gestures. The most used is :) (happy). Other emoticons include: L (sad), :o (surprised) or J (innocent).

Endorsement marketing – Getting another merchant or marketer to recommend you to his customers, with you offering a special discount available to his customers only.

End user – The person who uses the product, who may not be the same person who purchased the product. Example: toys are bought by parents but used by children.

Engagement – (1) Interacting with other people on social networks. (2) A strong interest in a product, technology, idea, or content for which a person has top-of-mind awareness and active pursuit of more knowledge.

Engraving – A printing process in which the ink is raised above the surface of the paper, giving the document a distinctive look and feel.

Evangelist – A consumer so enamored with and loyal to your product or brand that he proactively tells other people (friends, colleagues, associations, social media followers) why he loves the product and recommends others buy it too.

Envelope stuffer – Any promotional inserts enclosed with statements or invoices.

Evergreen – A promotion or ad campaign that is always current and effective regardless of the time of month, year, or decade it is used.

Event marketing – A marketing campaign centered on an event. The marketer may be the producer, promoter, or sponsor of the event. For instance, for its grand opening, a department store invited people in the neighborhood to a mini-fair held in the store's large parking lot. Booths offered a variety of free services, such as blood pressure measurement and ID bracelets for children.

Experiential marketing – Marketing that creates awareness for a brand by giving consumers a physical or digital interaction that is congruent with that brand. An example is Lipton iced tea, which advertises the brand as refreshing. Lipton has equipped some transit advertising (e.g., bus stops) with devices built into the freestanding structures that advertising the product. These devices spray a cooling mist that reinforces the Lipton brand message of relief from heat. Another example of experiential marketing is New York City's Times Square M&Ms store, which offers several interactive experiences. In one, visitors guess the number of M&Ms in a large clear globe. There is also an electronic machine that shows what color M&M best fits your mood based on your answers to a few questions.

Expire – A person whose subscription to a publication or service, or membership in an organization, has expired recently.

Expiration date – The date on which a special offer expires and is no longer available.

Extended Reality (XR) – Real-and-virtual combined environments and human-machine interactions generated by computer technology.

Eyeballs – The number of people who view a web page or online advertisement.

Eyebrow – A line of copy above the headline; also known as a pre-head; usually in bold italics and smaller type than the headline.

Exhibit – A company's booth at a trade show.

Exit pop – A window that pops up if visitors move to exit the page prematurely, without buying, downloading a white paper, registering for an event, or taking other actions the page is designed to generate. The window gets their attention and simply asks them to give their name and email address, often in exchange for a special report or another free gift given as the incentive for the visitor to fill in and submit their information.

Eye tracking – An optical device that records where the eye is looking in your ad or web page, how long it is looking at that element, and the sequence in which it scans or reads the document or screen.

F

F-pattern – A theory that visitors to a web page scan it in an F pattern, reading what is on the top and left side of the page first.

Factoid – A tiny sidebar in a document or web page containing a single concise fact or statistic.

Fanfold – A photo or illustration of multiple items (e.g., a set of free special reports) spread out to emphasize that the buyer is getting multiple bonuses.

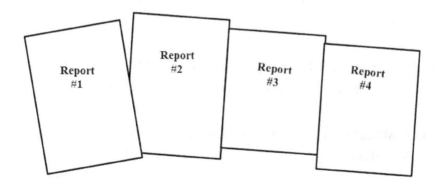

FAQ (frequently asked questions) – FAQ is a commonly used abbreviation for "frequently asked questions." The FAQ page on a website lists questions consumers ask the marketer most often and the answers.

Farm out – To assign work to an outside vendor rather than handle it in-house.

Fascination – A line of copy that engages the consumer's attention, arouses her curiosity, and makes her want to learn more. Example from Boardroom: "What never to eat on an airplane."

Fax broadcast – Mass distribution of advertising material to a list via facsimile machine.

Feature – Something a product is or has. For instance, a feature of a watering can is that it has a spout. The benefit is that it directs the water at the plant and not on the gardener.

Feature story – A full-length magazine article, ranging from 800 to 3,000 words or so. It can be written by the publication's staff or freelance writers or contributed by the marketer whose product or service is the topic of the article.

Federal Communications Commission (FCC) – Federal agency regulating broadcast and electronic communications.

Federal Trade Commission (FTC) – Federal agency regulating national advertising.

Fee – The charge made by an agency or advertising professional to the client for services performed.

Field – A space in an online form or record that holds one piece of data. On a landing page, the prospect's name is entered in one field, her email address in a second field, her phone number in a third field, and so on. The fewer fields you require the user to complete, the higher your conversion rate. For each additional field you require, the conversion rate drops about 10 percent. Therefore, you must strike a balance between high conversion rates vs. getting the data you need to qualify your prospect.

Firewall – A security barrier placed between an organization's internal computer network and the internet.

First-level connection – Someone you can send messages to directly on LinkedIn.

Firmographics – Characteristics of a business such as SIC, number of employees, location, and gross sales.

Fiverr – An online marketplace where advertisers can buy a number of advertising-related services (e.g., content writing, illustration, voice-over narration) starting for just $5.

Fixed field – A space in a record for a specific piece of information (e.g., last name) and allowing a maximum number of characters in the field.

Flame – An intentionally crude or abusive email message.

Flash – A rich media file format used to display animation on a web page. With the rising use of video, Flash has become less popular. Also, the Google algorithm does not rank pages done in Flash.

Flat file database – A simple list that is sorted in sequential order, with each record kept in the same format.

Floater – Similar to a pop-up or pop-under, except it is not blocked by pop-up blockers because it is part of the web page or landing page HTML code. The floater is used to capture the visitor's email address, usually by offering free content. It floats from one side of the screen to the center, where it blocks or covers what is being displayed on the web page the visitor was viewing; you can get rid of the floater usually by clicking an X in its upper-right corner. A floater is not blocked by the user's pop-up blocker because it is part of the HTML code used in the home page.

Flywheel – A model for business-to-business marketing featuring the 3-part inbound methodology of attract, engage, and delight the customer.[7]

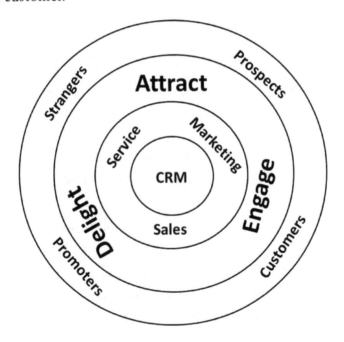

---

7 https://www.newbreedrevenue.com/blog/the-marketing-funnel-is-dead-and-the-flywheel-has-arrived

Focus groups – A market research technique in which an advertiser asks a small group of consumers for their opinion about the product and promotions for it.

Foil stamping – A printing process in which a gold or silver foil is affixed to the paper.

FOMO (Fear of Missing Out) -- A copywriting technique where you increase response rates by ratcheting up the sense of urgency, specifically by making prospects fear that if they don't reply to the ad immediately, the window of opportunity will close, and they will miss out on a great offer.

Font – A typeface; e.g., Times Roman, Courier. Fonts can be regular weight, italicized, boldface, or underlines.

Forecasting – Predicting inquiries, sales, or other performance metrics based on observation, judgment, and data.

Forms – The pages in most browsers that accept information in text-entry fields.

Four A's – American Association of Advertising Agencies, an industry trade association.

Four color – Artwork reproduced in full color using four basic inks: black, yellow, blue, red.

For position only (FPO) – An element in a layout that is not a final image but is merely a placeholder until the actual photograph or graphic is available. This is typically a stock photo used as a placeholder until the actual photo is taken.

Forum – A place on the internet where users come to discuss a topic of common interest.

Four U's – A formula invented by Mark Ford for writing headlines. It says a good headline is: (a) unique – you haven't heard it before, (b) useful – it contains a benefit, (c) ultra-specific – because specifics sell, and (d) urgent – because response increases when your ad has a sense of urgency.

Four-em quad – 36-point type size.

Fractional ad – An ad that takes less than a full page in a magazine or newspaper.

Freelance – A self-employed copywriter, photographer, artist, media buyer, or other advertising professional.

Free on free offer – Offering a free gift as an incentive to accept a free offer. For instance, I offer four free special reports to anyone who subscribes to my free e-newsletter. The reason to do so is it gets more people to accept the offer!

Freemium – While a premium is a free gift the prospect gets when he replies to your promotion, a freemium is a free gift sent to you with the promotion; it is yours whether you reply, buy, or not. Example: free mailing labels or rosary beads inside envelopes carrying fundraising letters; refrigerator magnets used in mailings aimed at homemakers.

Freemium app – A version of an app with limited functionality offered at no charge. The app owner makes money by upgrading and charging freemium users for premium features.

Free-standing insert (FSI) – An advertising flier or circular folded into a newspaper. The big advantage of FSIs is good color reproduction because images are printed on glossy stock. Even if the newspaper has color ads, the colors reproduce poorly on newsprint and tend to blur and lose focus.

Frequency – The number of times an ad is delivered to the same browser in a single session or time period. A site needs to use cookies to manage ad frequency. Or how often a customer makes purchases from a merchant. Or the number of times a person is exposed to an advertising message within a specified time period.

Friction – Resistance, lack of understanding, or distraction concerning your marketing claims and sales messages; difficulty using your website, shopping cart, or other e-commerce software; or confusion on how to order your product.

Frictionless commerce – The Facebook Discovery Commerce system helps enables frictionless commerce, enabling products to find people wherever they are. The system can help merchants anticipate shopper needs and then match products with the people most likely to love them.

Friend-get-a-friend (FGF) – A promotion containing two order forms or discount coupons, one for the recipient and a second for the recipient to pass along to a friend.

Fringe time – On television, time spots other than prime time.

Front end – The first product purchased by a new customer.

FTP (file transfer protocol) – A protocol that allows the transfer of files from one computer to another.

Fulfillment – The process of packing and shipping a product to a customer who has ordered it.

Fulfill and forget – You get an inquiry. The prospect doesn't seem a good fit for your business. But you're not sure. So, you fulfill their request for your catalog, brochure, product sample, or whatever else you offered in your promotion. You add the prospect to your database. But then you forget about them. You don't follow up because they are not a good lead. You have fulfilled their inquiry but given them no further attention beyond that.

Full-service agency – An ad agency that offers its clients a full range of advertising services including creative services, media buying, planning, marketing, and research – both online and offline.

Fundraising – Marketing that solicits donations for nonprofits.

G

G5 – The fifth-generation mobile network for smartphones, tablets, laptops, and other digital wireless communication. Data transfer rates on G5 networks are up to 10 gigabytes per second. Other advantages over earlier generations of mobile networks include more gaming and multimedia options, connectivity virtually everywhere with no "latency" (delays), and transfer of video and audio to other smartphones with no degradation in sound or picture quality. In addition, G5 networks feature high resolution, are easily manageable with the previous generations, broadband capacity to support more than 60,000 connections, and uniform, uninterrupted, and consistent connectivity across the world.

Gamification – Designing digital marketing, eLearning, and other online activities that incorporate elements of computer and video games; e.g., scoring, mazes, puzzles. The idea of gamification is to increase user engagement with marketing, learning, and other online activities.

Gated – Free content the consumer can get only if she fills out and submits a form online. The form is part of the landing page offering the freebie. At minimum, the form asks for the consumer's name and email address; other frequently requested information includes city, state, and phone number. The landing page captures the consumer's information, thus generating a lead online.

Gatefold – Folding a sheet of paper to form a brochure in which there are two flaps that can be opened from either side.

Garamond – A style of typeface like this.

General advertising – Advertising that seeks to instill a preference for the product in the consumer's mind, to promote the future sale of the product at a retail outlet or through a distributor or agent. This is the opposite of direct response advertising which seeks an immediate order.

General Data Protection Regulation (GDPR) – GDPR is a regulation that requires businesses to protect the personal data and privacy of EU citizens for transactions that occur within EU member states.

Generational marketing – Marketing that targets consumers by their age or generation.

Generation X – Anyone born between 1965 and 1980.

Generation Y – Anyone born between 1981 and 1996; also known as millennials.

Generation Z – Anyone born between 1997 and 2012.

Geocoding – Assigning geographic designations to name and address records.

Geodemographics – Appending Census data such as income, education, and type of home owned to a household file.

Geotargeting – The ability to target your pay-per-click ads and other marketing to prospects within a specific geographical area.

Ghostwriter – A writer who writes books, articles, speeches, or other material credited to another person; for instance, the writer who writes a speech given by the company CEO.

GIF (Graphics Interchange Format) – A data format for transmitting and displaying image and graphics.

Gimmick – A clever or out-of-the-ordinary technique used to draw attention to a promotion. For instance, to promote a defense system code-named The Gunfighter, the manufacturer hired an expert shooter to demonstrate quick-draw shooting (with blanks) in the booth.

Glicken – A Yiddish word, in marketing, it has come to mean a deal sweetener; a little something extra thrown in to sway the prospect and get him to buy.

Global Privacy Control (GPC) – An opt-out mechanism that allows consumers to delete personal information collected by companies in their customer database as well as disallow sales of that data to third parties.[8]

Glocal marketing – Doing local marketing that targets specific locations (e.g., zip codes, cities, counties, states, regions) on a global scale.

Glossy stock – Paper with a smooth and shiny surface. Most four-color printing is done on glossy stock, though there are flat stocks that can be used for color printing too.

---

8   Digital Daily News, 7/29/2021.

Google advertising – Pay-per-click ads you can buy on Google. The advertiser is charged every time someone clicks on the URL hyperlink in the ad. The Google ads must all conform to a standard word-length specification for headlines, descriptive text, and hyperlink URL as follows:

Field	Max length
Headline 1	30 characters
Headline 2	30 characters
Headline 3	30 characters
Description 1	90 characters
Description 2	90 characters
Path (2)	15 characters each

Google Analytics – A Google tool that measures key metrics tracking activity on your website.

Google Console – A tool that measures click-through rate, number of indexed pages, and number of dead links.

Google goulash – Articles written, usually by low-paid and minimally skilled writers, for purposes of giving a company greater visibility on search engines. The writers typically have little or no knowledge of or experience in the subject matter. They quickly create the article by Googling the topic, taking bits and pieces from half a dozen or so articles they find online, and cobbling them together into a new article. Google goulash articles have no new insights or advice and are just a relatively worthless rehash of already published content. No subject matter experts are interviewed by the writer to gain additional knowledge for the article.

Grading – Identifying people on your list by their quality and value as a prospect, based on the fact that not everyone is an equally valuable prospect or customer. We use the grading system of diamond, gold, silver, and copper to grade our prospects in descending order of quality from best to worst. We do not take on coppers as clients and seldom work with silvers. Almost all our clients are diamonds or gold.

Grammage – A measure of paper weight measured in grams per square meter.

Green marketing – Marketing that does not pollute or create waste. A cable TV commercial is green marketing, but direct mail is not. Also refers to marketing products that are environmentally friendly; e.g., a windmill farm instead of coal-powered generators.

Grid testing – Using a grid or table to test two variables (e.g., offer, mailing list) at a time in direct mail or email vs. testing a single variable in an A/B split test. In the grid, the horizontal axis represents one variable and the vertical axis the second variable. The rectangles in the grid are called test cells and are formed by the intersection of a row and a column. In each grid, we put the number of names being tested for the two variables.

Offer/Mailing List	List A	List B	List B
Offer 1	2,000 names	2,000	2,000
Offer 2	2,000	2,000	2,000
Offer 3	2,000	2,000	2,000

Gross profit margin – How much money you make on each sale. Calculated by taking the selling price of the product and subtracting the cost of making the product.

Gross rating points (GRPs) – The total number of homes viewing your commercials in a given market. To calculate GRP, multiply the number of times the commercial is aired times the percentage of the audience watching the commercial. Ten commercials with a 7 percent average share of audience have 70 GRPs.

Groupon – A site that offers free coupon codes that get consumers discounts on a large variety of merchandise and travel offers.

Guarantee – A seller's promise that the customer will be satisfied, and if not, may return the product for a refund or otherwise have the situation remedied; for a service, the provider may guarantee that they will redo the work at no additional charge if the customer is not happy with it.

Guerrilla marketing – A term coined by Jay Conrad Levison to describe marketing campaigns done on a shoestring, often using clever and creative strategies not used by big corporations and their ad agencies.

GUI (graphical user interface) – A screen for users to interact with and command the software to perform specific functions. Variables in GUI programming and design include calls to action, colors, page layouts, menu buttons, and content to make the software easier and more intuitive to use.

Gutter – The inside margins of two pages that face each other in a print publication.

H

Hack – To gain new customers through nontraditional marketing channels such as social media and blogging instead of traditional channels such as TV commercials and magazine advertising.

Halftone – A black and white photograph or illustration reproduced by using a series of black dots to create shades of gray as well as black.

Hard sell – Aggressive selling or marketing that puts the prospect under pressure to buy. When you call 800 numbers in some radio and TV commercials, the person who answers the phone is often compelled to give you the hard sell in his telemarketing script, saying whatever it takes to give him your credit card number. Also known as high-pressure selling; often practiced by salespeople who are on straight commission.

Hangout – A service that allows you to video chat with up to ten Google+ users at a time. During the chat, you can share content such as a Google Doc or YouTube video with others on the chat.

Hard bounce – An email that is undeliverable because of a bad address.

Hard offer – An offer where the consumer has to pay with check, credit card, money order, or PayPal when placing his order. The product is not shipped until payment is made.

Hashtag – A hashtag is a keyword phrase, written without spaces, with a # in front of it. Hashtags enable you and your audience to communicate about specific topics on social media networks.

Headline – A sentence in large, bold type at the top of the page in an ad, sales letter, or web page proceeding the text on the page.

Header tag – HTML code attached to a web page but not visible by users that clearly defines the page's purpose and theme. A header meta tag appears once on the site, on the homage page; these tags are used by search engine spiders to find and rank websites. Also called title tags or H1 tags.

H2 tag – Meta tags for the second-level pages on the site.

Heat mapping – A graphical representation of geographic data as it is applied to a specific metric; e.g., a heat map might show which regions of the country tend to buy more of your product than others.

Hero ingredient – In a dietary supplement, the most important ingredient (e.g., the most potent, the most unusual) used in the formulation. Advertising for supplements often features the hero ingredient as the major selling point.

Hit – When a page request is made, all elements or files that comprise the page are recorded as hits on a server's log file when a consumer views a website or page. If Dick visits your site five times and Jane visits once, you have six hits.

Home page – The page designated as the main point of entry of a website or the starting point when a browser first connects to the internet. When you go on a website, the first thing you see is the home page.

Horizontal market – A market consisting of a diverse group of consumers or businesses.

Host – A server connected to the internet (with a unique IP address) used to store website code, databases, applications, or other content. Hosting fees are usually charged by the server operator by the month.

Hosting, dedicated – A hosting service using an entire server dedicated to a single client's website.

Hotline – (1) Names on a mailing list of buyers who have purchased within the last 12 months. Based on the RFM formula, you get the best results mailing to hotline names. (2) Names on a mailing list of customers who have purchased recently, usually within the last 90 days. Hotline names usually work best because customers who have purchased most recently are also the most likely to purchase again. This is why there is a premium charge to rent just the hotline names from a list.

Hotlist – A list of potential customers for an offer generated prior to making the offer online. Often used to promote big events and product launches. One method of generating a hotlist is to invite people to a free webinar on the topic of the event or product launch; those who register become part of the hotlist.

House agency – A team of company employees that perform the functions of an ad agency though they are on staff with the marketer.

House file – A mailing list consisting of a company's active customers, inactive accounts, and prospects. Mailing to a house file typically produces many times more orders than mailing to a rented list. Also known as a house list.

House organ – A company-published newsletter or magazine.

HTML (hypertext mark-up language) – A coding language used to make hypertext documents for use on the Web. HTML emails can have photos and graphics vs. text emails that cannot. The HTML code determines the color, formatting, positioning, and layout of the web page or email.

HTTP (hypertext transfer protocol) – A standard method of publishing information as hypertext in HTML format on the internet.

HTTPS-SSL – HTTP with SSL (secure socket layer) encryption for security.

Hype (hyperbole) – Use of deliberate exaggeration in marketing.

Hyperlink – The clickable link in text graphics or images on a Web page that takes you to another place on the same page, another page, or a whole other site.

Hypertext – Electronic documents that present information that can be read by following many different directions through links, rather than just read linearly like printed text. Or text that includes hot links to other text, files, documents, or web pages.

I

Identification for advertisers (IDFA) – Unique code used by app developers to target and track ad performance across multiple devices.

Identity resolution – Building and maintaining databases of prospects based on multiple first, second, and third-party data sources. Purpose: To ensure you are reaching your best target prospects.

Image – The public's perception or impression of a firm or product.

Image Alt Text – Text displayed by some browsers when the mouse pointer hovers above an image. Alt text should incorporate your keywords and be no more than half a dozen words per image.

Impressions – A summary figure representing the total exposures of an advertising message in a given period of time, based on how many people have viewed it and how often they viewed it.

Impulse buy – A purchase made without deep consideration or thought.

Inactive customer – A customer who has not bought anything from you for at least 12 months or longer, or someone on an email list who has not opened any of your emails for 12 months.

In-app ads – Ads placed in your app page, so they periodically appear on the smartphone screen while you are using the app.

Inbound marketing – Marketing in which prospects come to you rather than you reaching out to them. Example: organic search.

Inbound telemarketing – You generate a phone call with a radio commercial or by other means, and when the prospect calls for more information, you try over the phone to sell them on buying your product.

Incentive – A free gift, discount, sweepstakes, contest, deadline, or other inducement to order now instead of later.

Inclusion marketing – Proactively making sure your marketing speaks respectfully, appropriately, and thoughtfully to the needs, beliefs, feelings, and aspirations of all of the many diverse communities that your company serves.

Indicia – A mark printed on an envelope that takes the place of postage stamps and allows the envelope to be mailed.

Industrial advertising – Advertising by manufacturers selling equipment, subassemblies, parts, and raw materials to other businesses. See www.marketing2engineers.com for more information.

In-house – Anything done internally within a company. In marketing, any marketing tasks performed by company employees as opposed to ad agencies, freelancers, and other vendors.

Industrial advertising – Advertising of industrial products and services typically sold to engineers, managers, purchasing agents, and other buying influences in manufacturing and process industries.

Influencer – A person who influences consumers to buy a particular brand through what seems to be unbiased and objective endorsements and recommendations. Influencers hypothetically support the brand without paid compensation or advertising. In reality, many influencers treat influencing as a business; they regularly approach brands and offer to give favorable reviews or other endorsements. In exchange, they ask for free products and services – and in some cases, money.

Infographic – A marketing document with facts and data pertaining to a particular topic related to the marketer's product or its application. Infographics are often on one side of an 8 ½ by 11-inch page with a combination of text and graphics, especially tables, lists, pie charts, bar charts, illustrations, and graphs. Information is presented in bite-sized chunks using multiple small sidebars. Infographics are posted on Pinterest and Instagram and usually hyperlink to the marketer's website or landing page.

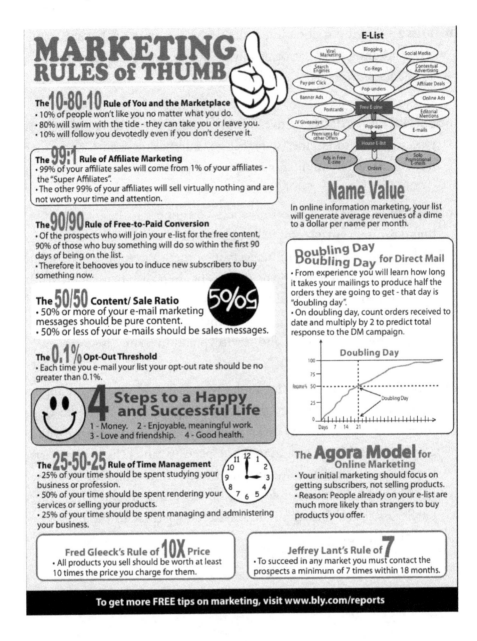

Infomercial – A long-form direct response TV commercial usually 30 minutes long and aired outside of prime time, such as early mornings and late night.

Information marketing – Selling e-books, paperbound books, webinars, seminars, videos, audios, and other information products over the internet.

Initial – A large letter placed at the beginning of a text for decorative purposes.

Inkjet printing – Small drops of ink are quickly sprayed onto a surface-finished grade of paper that quickly absorbs the ink.

In-page video ads – A video, usually two to three minutes in length, posted on a website, typically on the home page.

Inquiry advertising – Ads whose primary goal is to generate sales leads.

Inquiry fulfillment package – Product literature sent in response to an inquiry. Elements of an inquiry fulfillment package can include a cover letter, product brochure, company brochure, price sheet, reply form, and other inserts, such as article reprints and case studies. An inquiry fulfillment package can be paper sent through the mail or, more often, a PDF sent as an email attachment. Also known as an information kit.

Inquiry – A request for information made by a potential customer responding to an ad or promotion.

Insert – Promotional materials inserted in merchandise packages.

Insertion order – An agreement for a marketer to run an ad in a specific publication. The insertion order says which issue the ad is to run in and the size of the ad.

Inset photo – A small secondary photo on an ad or other page layout, separate from the larger main photo or illustration.

Instagram – A social network for posting graphics; similar to Pinterest. The design specifications between the two vary slightly, so you may have to alter your Pinterest graphic slightly before posting on Instagram.

Installment sales – You buy a product. But instead of paying the entire purchase price upfront, you pay it off in (usually) three or four monthly installments.

Integrated marketing communications – Marketing programs that integrate multiple strategies, channels, and media into a single cohesive campaign.

Intelligent Mail Barcode – A series of bars above the recipient's address when you get a piece of mail, implemented to improve efficiency and speed of delivery.

Intent data – Any information that enables you to predict buyer behavior and make a rough estimate of how likely a prospect is to buy your product. This can range from a pattern of buying products similar to your product to the prospect expressing strong interest in a survey.

Interactive advertising – Marketing that allows two-way communication between the advertiser and the consumer.

Interactive media – Media that facilitates two-way communication between the marketer and the consumer.

Internal link – A hyperlink that takes you to a page within the same website rather than to another website.

International Association of Business Communicators (IABC) – Trade association whose members are in corporate or marketing communications functions.

Internet – A collection of thousands of independent, interconnected networks providing reliable and redundant connectivity between disparate computers and systems by using common transport and data protocols. The internet has revolutionized marketing in several ways. First, by providing instant and cheap delivery of marketing messages and content via email. Second, by making it easy to find information on companies and products using a search engine to locate company websites. Third, with analytics software that provides a greater degree of tracking and measurement of marketing results much faster than with print or broadcast promotions.

Internet domain name – The unique name that identifies an internet entity. For instance, my website domain name is www.bly.com.

Internet marketing – Selling merchandise or information over the internet.

Internet radio – Live radio shows streamed over the internet.

Interruptive marketing – Advertising that stops someone in the middle of something they are doing to tell them about something they've expressed interest in and have not given you permission to send advertising messages to them. Examples include telemarketing calls that interrupt your dinner and email marketing messages from companies you do not know about products you don't care about.

Interstitial – An "intrusive" ad, often appearing near a hyperlink, which is spontaneously delivered without specifically being requested by a user.

Invoice stuffer – A promotional insert included in the envelope in which a bill is mailed to a consumer.

Involvement device – A physical device that shows through the window on the direct mail package's outer envelope, or an enclosed item of value that can be referred to in the outer envelope teaser. For subscription mailers, common involvement devices include tokens and stamps. Or it can be as simple as enclosing a balloon that the prospect is told to blow up. It's just something fun or interesting that gets the prospect to physically interact with the mailing piece.

IP address (Internet protocol address) – Every system connected to the internet has a unique IP address, which consists of a number in the format A, B, C, or D, where each of the four sections is a decimal number from 0 to 255.

Island position – A position on a page in a publication where an ad is entirely surrounded by articles and is not adjacent to any other ads.

ISP (Internet service provider) – A business that provides access to the internet.

Institutional advertising – Advertising that promote an institution or organization to create name recognition, goodwill, and favorable public opinion.

J

Java – An object-oriented programming language created by Sun Microsystems that supports enhanced features such as animation and real-time updating of information.

Jingle – Music and lyrics used in a commercial. On the TV series *Two and a Half Men*, Charlie Sheen played a jingle writer. Use of jingles has greatly declined in recent years, replaced by rock or pop music as the background sound.

Johnson box – A box at the top of a sales letter, above the salutation, containing a headline or introductory copy before the reader gets to the main body of the letter. In the pre-PC days, the Johnson box was laboriously typed by hand using asterisks. Today Microsoft Word can put an instant border around the words to make a Johnson box.

Journey, customer – The process or steps consumers go through in finding, evaluating, and ultimately purchasing a product.

JPEG (Joint Photographic Experts Group) – A method for compressing image files in RGB mode by up to 95 percent. JPEGs can display photographs and graphic images with millions of colors, compress well and are easy to download.

Jugular marketing™ – Marketing so riveting and compelling it "grabs you by the jugular" and won't let go until you respond.

Jumbo envelope – Oversized envelope measuring 9 by 12 inches.

Junk mail – A derogatory term for direct mail. The question has been raised that if direct mail is junk mail, shouldn't TV commercials be called junk TV?

#

Keyword-rich – Web pages and documents containing many references to the keywords for which you want to optimize your website.

Keeper – A premium or free bonus gift you are allowed to keep even if you return the product for a refund.

Kerning – In typography, the space between adjacent letters.

Key code – A code on a mailing label that identifies the list, test cell, and campaign the mail piece is from. If you affix the mailing label or imprint the key code on the reply element, you can track which list or test cell generated each reply you get.

Keyword – A word or phrase by which a web page or online document can be searched for and found. For instance, if you Google "direct response copywriter," my name and a description of what I do will come up on the Google search engine results page along with other websites also optimized for that keyword phrase.

Keyword stuffing – Overuse of keywords in website copy and meta tags with the mistaken belief that it will raise your search engine rankings – it won't.

Keyword meta tag – A list of keywords on a page's meta tags. Google once gave weight to these but now ignores them.

Kicker – If you return the product for a refund, you must also return the kicker premium with it; you are not allowed to keep the free bonus gift if you do not keep the product.

Kraft – Paper stock with a brownish-orange hue.

KLT – A marketing principle that says the more your prospects know, like, and trust you, the more likely they are to buy from you.[9]

---

9   Carline Anglade-Cole, email, 8/1/21.

L

Laminate – To bond a plastic film to a printed sheet using heat and pressure. The laminate protects the sheet from wear and damage. When I wrote sales sheets aimed at oil rig workers, we laminated them, otherwise, the oil on their hands would destroy the sheets.

Landing page – Any web page designed to generate conversion or other direct action, as opposed to a page that just provides content or links to more content. In the landing page below, the prospect has to fill in her information to download a free marketing handbook.

Launch – A coordinated, and often big marketing campaign to introduce a new product to the market, with the objective to generate a large sales volume in a short period of time, typically a couple of days to a week.

Layout – The design of a promotion, including headline, body copy, illustrations, photographs, logo, and any other elements, all positioned where the marketer wants them.

Lead – See also *Sales lead*; an inquiry from a person who is a potential customer for your product or service.

Lead generation – Any marketing activity that produces sales leads.

Lead magnet – A special report or other free content given to give prospects an incentive to respond to your offer. Ideally, the contents of the lead magnet are related to your product or business, so that reading it encourages prospects to want to do business with you. Also called a bait piece.

Lead nurturing – Communicating, often for an extended period, with the lead until they finally buy something and become a customer. Lead nurturing messages can be emails, postal letters, or phone calls, or any combination. In a series of lead nurturing messages, some of the messages sell the product while others educate prospects with content relating to the product or the problem it solves.

Lead rating system – Classifying leads based on how likely they are to become customers. I rate leads (from best to worst) diamond, gold, silver, and copper. A diamond is a highly desirable potential customer we would do almost anything to have. A copper is so suboptimal that we fulfill their inquiry but do no further follow-up.

Lead scoring – A quantitative method of assessing lead quality based on prospects' behavior and data. The score rates each lead on the probability of closing the sale, which helps marketing and sales determine which leads should be followed up more proactively.

Leading – The space between lines of type.

Leave-behind – A brochure, catalog, product sample, or other material a salesperson leaves with the prospect when departing.

Left-brain advertising – Ads that appeal to logic and the rational mind.

Letterset – A printing process in which the elevated sections are inked up and in the process deposit some of the ink on the paper to be printed.

Lettershop – A firm that reproduces, assembles, and mails direct mail packages. Their services may include printing, personalization, addressing envelopes, affixing postage, placing the elements of the package in the envelope in the proper order, and taking the mailing to the post office. Also called a mailing house.

Lifetime customer value (LCV) – The amount of money a person spends with you during the period they are an active customer. For instance, if the average customer spends $100 a month and stays with you for three years, LCV is $3,600. Many marketers make the error of basing their customer acquisition cost on the price of the first purchase, so if the initial order is $100, they only want to spend $20 or $30 on marketing to get that customer. Smarter marketers base their customer acquisition cost on LCV. So, if the LCV is $3,600, they can afford to spend hundreds of dollars to acquire a new customer. Knowing LCV, therefore, gives you a huge advantage because you can afford to spend more on customer acquisition than your competitors.

Lift letter – Also called a lift note or publisher's letter, this is a second letter included in a direct mail package; the lift letter is designed to increase response to the mailing. Also known as a publisher's letter because it was at one time primarily used in mailings that solicit magazine subscriptions. Another name for it is the lift note. Typically, the lift note is printed either on letter size or Monarch size paper.

Licensing – An arrangement where you let some other firm sell your product or use your technology or intellectual property in exchange for a fee, usually a dollar amount on each unit sold.

Line engraving – A plate for letterpress printing created by etching on the basis of a line original.

Line extension – Taking the brand name of a successful product and putting it on a new product you plan to introduce.

Link – An electronic connection between two destinations on the web. A link in an email or online ad usually takes you to a web page. A link on a web page usually takes you to another web page, either in the same site or a different site.

Link-bait – A page on your website that's so interesting that other websites and blogs provide their visitors with links to your page. A large number of these inbound links raises your site's ranking in the search engines.

Link building – The activity of getting other websites to link to your website, with the objective being to improve your search engine rankings.

LinkedIn – A social network primarily oriented toward business professionals who are looking for either prospects or a job.

LinkedIn, first-level connection – People you are directly connected to on LinkedIn. You have accepted their invitation on LinkedIn, or they have accepted yours. You can send them a message directly on LinkedIn.

LinkedIn, second level connection – People connected to your first-level LinkedIn connections. You can send an invite for them to become a first-level connection by clicking Connect, or you can use LinkedIn InMail.

LinkedIn, third-level connection – People connected to your second-level LinkedIn connections. Your ability to send invites is more limited than with second-level connections.

LinkedIn, out-of-network – People not connected to any of your first, second, or third level connections.

LinkedIn InMails – With a premium account, you can send messages to people you are not connected to.

Link farm – A set of web pages created with the sole aim of linking to a target page in an attempt to improve that page's search engine ranking.

List – Names and addresses of consumers or companies available for direct marketing campaigns on the commercial list rental market.

List broker – A person who rents mailing lists. You do not pay an extra fee to rent mailing lists from a broker. The list broker gets his profit as a sales commission from the list owner, so you do not pay anything extra when you rent from a broker vs. renting directly from the owner. When you need a list, you should always go through a list broker rather than a list owner or manager. Reason: the list owner or manager has a profit motive for getting you to rent his list, regardless of whether it's the best list for your campaign. The list broker has a financial incentive (repeat orders) for getting you lists that work rather than pushing any particular list from you.

List compiler – A person or company that compiles names and addresses from directories, public records, newspapers, websites, and other sources for identifying a group of people who have something in common; e.g., they all drive BMWs.

List hygiene – Updating or removing incorrect or incomplete data from the fields and records in the database. List cleaning also involves correcting any inaccurately formatted data in fields; for instance, customer accounts missing the bank prefix.

List manager – A company that proactively markets a mailing list to direct mail and email marketers on behalf of the list owner in exchange for a commission. Companies with large lists may have the list manager on staff as an employee.

List owner – The company or person that owns a given mailing list. Agora Publishing, for instance, is the owner of the subscriber lists for its various newsletters.

Listserve – A program that automatically sends email to a list of subscribers. It is the mechanism that is used to keep specific groups informed. The Listserve is the group of people who have signed onto the list to get the messages.

List segmentation – Allowing direct marketers to select portions of a list for direct mail or email marketing based on a demographic, psychographic, or other selection factor. Done correctly, list segmentation almost always generates a boost in response rates.

List rental – Paying a fee to mail your promotion to someone's list one time.

List swap – Company A uses Company B's mailing list without paying a rental fee for it. In exchange, Company B mails to Company A's list without paying for it. But the swap is a one-time event, not a permanent trade. And it is for an equal number of names from both lists.

Lithography – Any printing process where the printing areas of the plate lie on the same place as the non-printing parts.

Live stamp – An actual postal stamp affixed to a direct mail envelope. Using live stamps usually produces a better response than a postage meter or mailing indicia.

Load – Usually used with upload or download, it means to transfer files or software – to "load" – from one computer or server to another computer or server.

Local search – Searching for businesses and websites within a specific geographic range; e.g., TV repair shows in Morris County, NJ.

Log or log files – Files that keeps track of network connections.

Login – The identification or name used to access – long into – a computer, network, or site.

Logo – The name of a company or brand set in specially designed lettering.

Look-a-like or Lookalike Audience – Facebook users with similar demographics and psychographics to the people already on your e-list, which Facebook then targets with your ads. See also *Retargeting*.

Long tail keywords – These are actually keyword phrases with multiple words, and they are very specific. "Cars" is a short tail keyword. "1957 Pontiac Indian Chief with V8 engine" is a long tail keyword. Long tail keywords, being narrow in focus, tend to attract more qualified prospects. And you can buy the clicks with a PPC ad campaign at a lower cost than the more competitive short tail keywords; e.g., "beer" costs more than "imported German dark brown lager."

Loss leader – A product the marketer prices so low, he makes no money or even loses money on the sale. The objective is to get a new customer by offering her a great bargain.

Lottery – In a lottery, winners are chosen by chance and must make a purchase to enter.

Loyalty program – The more your customer buys your product or service, the better they get treated, usually with gifts, discounts, and perks. Example: frequent flier miles that entitle some customers to use the airline's lounge at the airport and give free upgrades to first class.

Low-hanging fruit – Those consumers who are easiest to sell to and most likely to buy your product for one reason or another; e.g., they own and are happy with an earlier model which is aging and therefore needs to be replaced.

Lumbeck system – Uses polyvinyl acetate adhesive binding to glue the pages of a brochure or other multi-page printed piece.

Lumpy envelope – Enclosing a three-dimensional item in the envelope, such as a ballpoint pen or tea bags, to make the envelope lumpy. The recipient sees and feels that there is an object inside the envelope and is compelled to open the envelope to find out what's in it.

M

Machine insertion – Using machines to insert, in the right order, the multiple elements of a direct mail package into the envelope.

MAD (money, authority, desire) – An acronym to describe a qualified prospect as someone with the money, authority, and desire to buy your product.

Madison Avenue – The mainstream of the New York City advertising community. Madison Avenue is a street that runs along the East Side of Manhattan but used in the advertising sense, the term "Madison Avenue" refers to ad agencies located in the heart of midtown Manhattan.

Magalog – A direct mail piece designed to look like a magazine.

Mailing list – A list of names and addresses that is used in direct mail or email marketing. Thousands of such lists can be rented by direct marketers and online marketers. The usual minimum quantity of names you can rent is 5,000.

Make good – To rerun an ad at no charge to the advertiser because the publication made a mistake in its reproduction, placement, or timing; for instance, a sporting goods store takes out an ad in the sports section, and the newspaper runs it in the movie review section.

Mail monitoring – Tracking methods that determine how long it takes individual pieces of mail to reach their destinations and whether they were delivered at all.

Mail order – Traditionally, the consumer gets a direct mail package or sees an ad, responds by ordering a product, and the advertiser delivers the product by mail. Nowadays refers to any one-step marketing.

Mail order advertising – Ads whose primary goal is to generate orders.

Mail order rate – A lower rate for advertising in a newspaper or magazine offered to mail order marketers; brand marketers pay the regular rate, which is higher.

Mail plan – A written plan for a direct mail marketing campaign.

Mailer – Any organization or individual who uses direct mail.

Mailing list – An online mailing list is an automatically distributed email message on a particular topic going to certain individuals.

Map pack – The section of the Google search engine result page that displays businesses sought in a local search; for instance, if you search "dry cleaners Bergen county," the map pack will list the dry cleaners in that county.

Marcom – Short for marketing communications, which is what corporate America calls advertising, PR, and promotion; any communication that helps market a product.

Margin – The amount or percentage by which the selling price of an item exceeds the seller's or manufacturer's cost of goods.

Market – A portion of the population representing potential and current customers for a product or service.

Market basket analysis – Determining which products or services customers purchase together; e.g., people who buy burgers also buy fries.

Market research – A survey or other research to gauge consumer sentiment toward a brand or understand consumer behavior surrounding purchase of a particular product or product category.

Marketing communications – Communications used in marketing a product or service. Marketing communications – "marcom" for short – includes advertising, public relations, online marketing, and sales promotion.

Marketing – The activities companies perform to produce, distribute, promote, and sell products and services to their customers. Marketing encompasses four activities known as the Four Ps: product, price, place (distribution), and promotion. The general public sees marketing as synonymous with the last P, promotion.

Marketing automation – Software that automatically implements the delivery of messages in a marketing campaign. Emails are sent according to a predetermined schedule. The system reminds marketing staff when to make telemarketing calls, send postcards, and deliver other marketing tactics.

Marketing database – A database of customers, their buying history and habits, and their demographic and psychographic characteristics.

Marketing penetration – Percentage of people on a list or in a given area who are buyers.

Marketing plan – A written document outlining the schedule of planned marketing activities for the year and the rationale and strategy behind them. The plan spells out your marketing strategy (how you intend to market your product).

Marketing visibility – A measure of reach (how far and wide your marketing presence extends) and regularity (how often your brand and message are visible to your target audience).[10]

Mark-up – The practice of a marketing agency adding cost to a service purchased on behalf of a client; e.g., if an ad agency pays an illustrator $500 for a drawing to be used in a client's brochure, they might bill the client $600 – a 20 percent mark-up. The mark-up is mainly compensation for doing the work of looking for a supplier and supervising the service being purchased for the client. It also compensates the agency for laying out their cash upfront to buy the item.

Market share – The percentage of totals sales in a product category accounted for a particular product or brand; e.g., Coca-Cola has a 17.8 percent share of the market for cola drinks.

Mashup – Content made from multiple types of media drawn from pre-existing sources to create a new work.

---

10   GlobalSpec Marketing Maven, 8/5/2021.

Maslow's Hierarchy of Needs – A theory that in practical marketing application means that consumers are motivated to buy or take other actions to satisfy needs and wants on five levels. From the lowest to the highest, these categories of needs are physiological (e.g., staying healthy, having food and shelter); safety (e.g., being secure and protected from harm or threats); love; self-esteem (i.e., feeling good about oneself); and self-actualization (i.e., living up to your full potential; working toward, achieving, and attaining the things that matter most to you). Your customers typically, but not always, strive to satisfy the lower levels of the Hierarchy of Needs (e.g., physical, safety, and security); once they meet those needs, they move up the hierarchy and act to fulfill the higher levels. However, this is not universally true; some consumers who lack the buying power to satisfy a major physiological need, such as having a roof over one's head or food on the table, will buy products that address needs higher up in the hierarchy. These products are often premium merchandise (e.g., a $400 pair of athletic shoes). Owning premium products at this level makes them feel good, even happy, without solving more major issues.

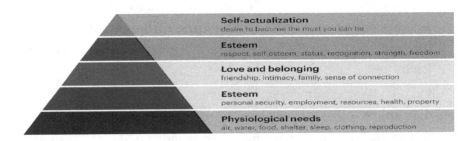

Mass advertising – Advertising aimed at the general public.

Matte finish – Dull paper finish that has no gloss.

Matures – Anyone born between 1922 and 1945.

Mechanical – Type and artwork pasted up on a board for reproduction by the printer.

Media – Any method of communication that brings information, entertainment, and advertising to the public or the business community.

Media kit – Material publishers send to marketers to get them to advertise in their publication. The media kit is either a hard copy, PDF, or posted online in HTML. Elements of a hard-copy media kit include a folder, sample issue, rate card, audit statement, and editorial calendar.

Media buyer – Person who buys ad space and air time in various media including magazines, newspapers, TV and radio shows, and online.

Member get a member – Offering a customer an incentive, such as a free gift or product discount, for recommending you to a friend or colleague. For instance, if I bring three new members to my local gym, I get the next month of my membership free.

Membership site – A website you can access only by paying a monthly subscription fee. When you join the site, you can access products, content, and services on the site. For an example, see my membership site www.infoproductcentral.com.

Meme – A thought, joke, idea, or concept, usually an image with text, to be shared online.

Merchant account – An account that allows you to take credit card orders.

Merchandising – Activities designed to promote the sale of goods in retail stores or catalogs.

Merge-purge – To merge multiple mailing lists together and purge the newly created master list of duplicate records or names. That way, you avoid sending multiple copies of your mailing to people who appear on more than one of the lists. (See also *De-dupe.*)

Message windows – Small windows that pop up on your screen containing brief messages or alerts.

Meta data – A collection of data so large it cannot easily be processed or manipulated by your computer.

Meta tags – Words or phrases embedded within the HTML code used to create websites. Meta tags almost always contain keywords that help search engines find and rank the page. The meta tags are "behind" the text and graphics on the page and therefore aren't normally visible to the casual visitor. To view the meta tags on any website, choose the View menu from your browser's toolbar. Then click on Source. A window will open, revealing the meta tag HTML text.

The title meta describes the topic of the web page. The descriptive meta tag is what the user sees when your site comes up in the Google search engine results page during a keyword search.

Metaverse – A shared digital world built using virtual reality and augmented reality. Facebook founder Jeff Zuckerberg describes the metaverse as a virtual environment where you can be present with people in digital spaces[11] and predicts the metaverse will be the successor to the mobile internet.[12]

---

11   Infinite Scroll, "Facebook Wants Us to Live in the Metaverse," Kyle Chayka, 8/5/2021.

12   IAB SmartBrief, 7/29/2021.

Millennials – A person born between 1981 and 2000; according to Google, nearly half of B2B buyers are Millennials.

Microblogging – Blog entries of 200 characters or less. Twitter is the largest microblogging social media network.

Micro-copy – Small website elements that, when executed well, can improve the user experience and help make it easier for your visitors to do what they want to do and to find what they want to find. Micro-copy elements include menu buttons, banners, pop-ups, instructions, calls to action, and page headers.

Microsite – A small, simple website dedicated to a single product.

Mime – A method of encoding a file for delivery over the internet.

MiniBuk®, – A small, undersized book with a trim size of about 3 1/2 by 5 1/2 inches. MiniBuks are underused today, so the novelty of publishing your content in this format can make it stand out.

Minimum viable outcome – For a pilot program launching a product or service, the smallest scope for your pilot that will still create an outcome your customers will be happy with.

Minimum viable product – In product development, the product with the highest return on investment vs. risk.

Mission statement – A brief statement describing why an organization exists and what it hopes to achieve going forward while articulating its nature, values, and business.

Mix and match – Making sure all the personalized elements of a direct mail package match; i.e., preventing John Jones's letter from being placed in an envelope with Jack Johnson's personalized order form.

Mix modeling – Correlates spikes in spending on various marketing channels to spikes in product revenues to determine which markets contribute the most to sales; also known as econometric modeling.

Mixed reality (MR) – An environment created by computers where physical and virtual objects co-exist and interact in real time.

Mobile-Friendly – A website or email that is easy to read when displayed on a smartphone. Google now penalizes websites that are not mobile-friendly by lowering their ranking on the search engine.

Mobile marketing – Marketing campaigns – mainly websites and emails – that specifically target users of mobile devices, including smartphones and tablets.

Mobile wallet – A "virtual wallet" where credit card information is stored on mobile devices, enabling users to buy retail or online using their smartphones.

Mock-up – A rough layout showing how a finished promotion will appear. Mock-ups are created to get approval from those who must approve your marketing piece before it is printed, posted, or mailed.

Modem – A contraction for "modulation/demodulation," it is the device that converts a digital bit stream into an analog signal (and back again) so computers can communicate across phone lines.

Modeling – Analyzing a customer database to create a profile of the ideal customer, the person most likely to buy.

Module – Just as books are written in chapters, courses, seminars, and training programs are usually organized into distinct modules, each covering a specific subtopic in the training program.

Monarch envelope – Small wedding invitation-size envelope measuring 3 7/8 by 7 ½ inches.

Monetary – How much money a customer spends with you in a given period of time.

Monetize – To make money from marketing or another activity. For instance, marketers are looking for ways to better monetize their activity on Facebook and Blab.

Money shot – The most important, dramatic, and climactic scene in a movie, TV show, or commercial; the most dramatic and memorable shot.

MP3 – A file format used to stream audio over the internet.

MP4 – A file format used to stream video over the internet.

Multibuyer – A customer who has bought from a merchant two or more times, preferably within a reasonably brief period.

Multichannel marketing – Using two or more different marketing channels (e.g., direct mail, telemarketing, email) in a coordinated campaign. Forrester Research reports that "marketers who have adopted multichannel marketing practices have realized significant business benefits ranging from improved campaign performance to higher return on marketing investments." Of marketers surveyed by Forrester, 77 percent agree they will drive more sales and profits by evolving into an effective multichannel marketing company. Other benefits of multichannel marketing, as reported by Forrester, include increased impressions, higher conversion rates, and improved campaign ROI.

Multicultural marketing – Marketing targeting subcultures whose members hold beliefs, values, customs, and other cultural characteristics – including race, ethnicity, nationality, and religions – that differentiate them from the mainstream of society.

Mustache – A brief line of copy, often italicized, appearing below the headline; also called a post-head.

N

NAICS (North American Industrial Classification System) – A system of identifying industries by a code with three to six digits, replacing the old Standard Industrial Code.

Name squeeze page – A landing page, usually brief, designed to capture the user's email address, either in exchange for an offer of free content or as a condition of allowing the reader access to copy on a landing page or other Web page. (Also known as a squeeze page.)

Nano-writing – Short copy written for **chat bots,** typically 300 words or less.

Native advertising – Ads deliberately written and designed to look like articles, also known as editorial style advertising. The idea is that consumers respond better to editorial matter than they do to advertising, so you can increase response by making your ad look like editorial material. Many publications require you to place in small type the word "Advertisement" at the top of native ads.

Native in-feed ads – Native ads that match the look and feel of your content. Native in-feed ads are usually placed in between the content of your feed or where your feed begins or ends. As visitors scroll down your content, they encounter in-feed ads.

Native commerce – Marketing that is relevant to what publishers are already writing about and matches the type of products that are typically discussed on their site, making it a seamless experience for the readers. Native commerce can also integrate an e-commerce platform right into the user experience so that a reader can go from reading your site to shopping the content without being redirected to a third-party site.

Navigation – The ability on the web to move from page to page or site to site, usually achieved with click buttons and hyperlinks.

NCOA (National Change of Address) – A service of the U.S. Postal Service where a list is run against a database to update the addresses of people on the list who may have moved. The average American moves 11 times in his or her lifetime.

Negative ad campaign – An ad campaign that focuses primarily on bashing the competition. Used mainly, but not exclusively, in political advertising.

Negative option – In a continuity program, saying "no" to the current month's selection, so the seller does not send it. Monthly shipments continue automatically unless and until you say you don't want them anymore.

Nesting – Fitting one piece of printed promotional material inside another, usually in a direct mail package.

Netiquette (internet etiquette) – The rules of how to behave on the internet.

Netizen – An active internet user.

Net name rental agreement – When renting multiple lists from a broker under such an arrangement, you pay for each name only once. In other words, if Joe Jones should show up on three of the lists you rent, you are charged for his label just once.

Neural networks – A data analysis method used to discover and predict relationships in the data that cannot be detected by other algorithms.

Net Promoter Score (NPS) – A metric that measures a customer's willingness to recommend a product service to others; NPS measures intent, but not purchase or other consumer action.

Newbie – A term to describe anyone new to an area, but especially someone new to internet marketing; also called a noob.

Newsgroup – A discussion group on Usenet devoted to talking about a specific topic.

New movers – Consumers who have recently moved into a new neighborhood. Lists of new movers can be particularly responsive because the new movers need to buy a lot of stuff for their new home and need to find new service providers (e.g., gas station, dry cleaner, pharmacy, grocery store, restaurant, dentist) because in moving they have left their old suppliers behind.

Newspaper preprint – An advertising insert that looks like part of the newspaper but is actually produced and sponsored by an advertiser; the preprint is usually inserted in the Sunday edition of the newspaper.

Newsprint – The cheap paper stock, containing a high wood pulp content, on which newspapers are printed.

Niche – A segment of a market, industry, or activity; e.g., copywriting is an activity; writing copy about financial services is a niche within copywriting. Other examples of niches include stock market investing, option trading, running, weight loss, diabetes, and muscle cars.

Nielsen rating – The percentage of U.S. households watching a network program.

Nixie – A direct mail piece that cannot be delivered because the recipient's address on the mailing label is incorrect. If you mail first class, your nixies will be returned to you; if you mail third class, they won't.

Non-pay – A customer who gives you an invalid credit card number or a bad check and who doesn't respond to your collection efforts is a non-pay.

Nth name – When renting a mailing list, if you are only mailing to part of the list, you can select to mail to every nth name only; that is, every fifth name, seventh name, etc. If a list has 100,000 names and you are renting 20,000 names, you will mail to every fifth name.

No-code platform – Templates that you can use to modify existing artificial intelligence programs for your own purposes, typically automating simple tasks, such as customer tracking or schedule management.

Non-fungible token (NFT) – An NFT[13] is a verifiable digital token that represents your ownership of an asset on a "blockchain" – a database[14]

---

13 Kiplinger, 5/6/2021.
14 Investopedia, 8/2/2021.

---

that stores data in blocks. NFTs can be used to buy and sell digital images. "Non-fungible" name means that NFTs cannot be replaced or exchanged with one another.

Nostalgia marketing – When brands that have been around a long time go back in their archives and rerun classic ads that have become cultural icons (e.g., Jolly Green Giant, Janitor in a Drum, Wesson Oil, Shake & Back Chicken) or reuse the characters or sales themes from those ads in new marketing campaigns.

Not-for-profit rates – Lower postage rates paid by nonprofits.

No-pay – A person who orders a product and then does not pay for it. Also called a delinquent account.

Number 10 envelope – Standard size business envelope measuring 4 1/8 by 9 ½ inches.

O

O2O – Offline to online marketing; e.g., sending out a direct mail piece or running a print ad where the call to action sends people to a website or landing page to request a lead magnet.

Opt-in – When users give you their name and email address along with permission to send email messages to them.

OEM (original equipment manufacturer) – A company that manufactures a product rather than sourcing it.

Offer – What the prospect gets when he responds to your promotion, combined with what he has to do to get it. Example: "Fill in your name and email address to download our free white paper."

Offer threshold –A term coined by Dan Kennedy, threshold is a qualitative measure of the degree of consumer resistance to acting on an offer. A high threshold has the greatest resistance because it requires consumers to do something that may put them in an uncomfortable situation; e.g., sitting through a timeshare sales pitch. A low threshold offer is downloading a white paper with only a couple of simple fields to fill out and none of them asking for sensitive information.

Off-the-page advertising – Ads that attempt to generate a direct order for the product rather than generate inquiries or build brand awareness. Very few people today know how to write and design off-the-page ads that are profitable.

Official mailing – A direct mail package designed to look like a government communication or other official notice. Some marketers make the mailing look like an IRS notice, but this is a bad strategy because it frightens the consumer, thus causing resentment against you.

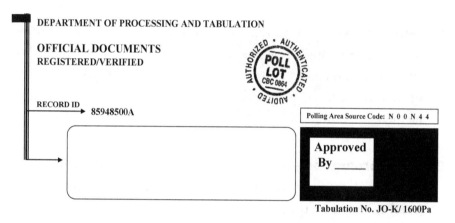

Offset printing – A lithographic printing process used by small local print shops to print resumes, fliers, and other simple documents. The printing form transfers the image onto a blank cylinder, which in turn prints onto the paper.

Omnichannel marketing – All the different ways retailers market to customers: online, offline, and in-store.

Onboarding – (1) The process of entering and moving a customer through a sales funnel. (2) Integrating a new employee into your team and corporate culture.

Onboarding, ecommerce – The process of engaging new opt-in subscribers and website visitors with tactics that include content marketing, email, and social media. The goal is to build engagement so that the subscribers climb the ladder from casual opt-in to active reader to qualified prospect to first purchase to regular customer.

One-click ordering – The customer can make a purchase online with a single mouse click, bypassing the shopping cart. This requires that her information, such as address and credit card, has been previously entered on the site.

One-page website – A website in which the content, instead of being presented in multiple pages, is all on one long home page. Instead of clicking on a menu to find the page with the content you want, you just go to the home page and start scrolling down – everything will be there.

One-step promotion – Marketing that generates an order direct from the promotion. Example: an infomercial where you call the toll-free number and order the product.

One-Time Offer (OTO) – A product offer you make to people, usually those who have just subscribed to your e-zine or joined your e-list, that they will see once and not again.

On spec – Creating a marketing communication without pay or the promise that the client will use it, done in the hopes of winning business from that client. Generally, an unwise practice.

Onionskin paper – A glazed, wood-free, translucent paper.

Online course – A web-based course

Opacity – The degree of a paper's resistance to light. Papers are made more opaque with wood, kaolin, talcum, and titanium dioxide.

Open rate – Percentage of recipients who open the email you send them.

Operational database – Used to process transactions and produce monthly statements.

Opportunity seekers – A market of people looking for small businesses and schemes to make money, usually working at home as their own boss.

Opt in – To agree to receive promotional emails when registering on a particular website from the site owner and other companies to whom he or she may rent your email address.

Opt out – To request that an e-list owner take your name off the list or at least make sure you are not sent any promotional emails.

Order form – A piece of paper or online page the prospect can fill out and submit or return to you to order your product.

Order page – When you click the Order Now button on a landing page, you are taken to an order page describing the offer and allowing you to place your order online.

Organic search – When a free search engine finds web pages based on a user initiating a keyword search and displays those links when a user searches for information on the particular topic of the page.

Other Peoples' Networks (OPN) – E-lists, newsletter subscribers, websites, and other online methods through which other marketers target the same market as you. Getting these other people to give you access to their OPN vs. affiliate programs, JV partnerships, and other online tactics is a fast and virtually free way to add customers on OPN's to your e-list.

Over-the-top (OTT) – A service that bypasses cable, broadcast, satellite television, and other platforms that control the distribution of video content and instead offers streaming video directly to users via the internet.

Outbound links – Links from your site to pages on other people's websites. While the hyperlink to reach these outside pages can appear anywhere on your site, you should have a separate links page where the bulk of your outbound hyperlinks are posted.

Outbound marketing – Any marketing where you have to reach out to your prospects rather than them coming to you. Examples: email marketing, ads, direct mail.

Outbound telemarketing – Renting a list of names and cold calling them to sell them a product.

Outcome – The result your customer achieves by using your product or service. For instance, if you are a criminal lawyer, the outcome your clients want is to be found not guilty. Marketing that talks about outcomes instead of features and benefits can often be very effective. For instance, if you offer SEO services, don't talk about details like meta tags; tell prospects how much more traffic you can get them.

Outdoor advertising – Billboards, signs, kiosks, and any other ads appearing outdoors.

Outer envelope – The envelope containing all the elements of a direct mail package.

Out of home (OOH) – Out of home is advertising that can be found outside of the consumer's home; examples include billboards, bus shelters, benches, and skywriting.

Overlay – Adding additional information to records in a database; for example, if you have a list of business customers, you can run it through a file of business addresses and add those addresses to your database.

Owned, earned, and bought – Owned media are your web properties like blogs, websites, and landing pages; earned media is essentially online word of mouth, such as retweets and reposts; bought media is paid advertising like Google AdWords.

P

Package – The full set of elements in a direct mail promotion; e.g., the outer envelope, letter, brochure, lift note, buck slip, brochure, order form, and reply envelope.

Package goods – Products wrapped or packaged by the manufacturer. Package goods are low in cost and typically sold on store shelves.

Package stuffer – Advertising fliers placed into the outgoing packages containing products ordered by consumers. The consumer opens the box to get what he ordered and finds stuffers promoting (usually) related offers from other marketers. Also called a package insert.

Page – All websites are a collection of electronic "pages" formatted in HTML.

Page views – Number of times users request a page.

Package insert – A sales flier, order card, or other promotional piece selling a product that is shipped to you along with a product you ordered.

Packaging – The copy and design used on the box or package the product comes in when displayed in stores or shown on TV or in ads.

Pad – When your copy comes up short of the required word length, you may add extra content of questionable value just to make the word length. This is called padding; high school and college students have been known to do this with term papers.

Paid circulation – A magazine which the reader has paid to subscribe to.

Paid media – Media exposure that you have to pay for; e.g., newspaper advertising; also called bought media.

Paid search – Paid advertising on Google and other search engines so that your page or site comes up in a keyword search for that topic. Also called pay-per-click (PPC) advertising.

Pampered consumer – Any customer who is pampered with information, options, and assistance throughout their purchase lifecycle. Pampered consumers expect merchants to put them at the center of the merchant's commerce operation.[15]

Pandora – A social online radio station that allows users to create their own stations based on their favorite artists and types of music.

Pantone – A color system used by graphic artists and others to select the desired colors to be used in a design or coating; today, over 1,000 Pantone colors are available.

Paperboard – A printing material stiffer and stronger than paper but thinner than cardboard.

---

15   Sitecore

Pareto principle – A theorem that 80 percent of your orders will come from 20 percent of your customers; 80 percent of your leads will come from 20 percent of your marketing; and in all activities, 80 percent of results come from 20 percent of your activity or effort.

Pass-along circulation – A publication's audience of readers who do not subscribe or buy it at a newsstand or bookstore. They typically get the publication either at the library or from a subscriber who "passes it along" to them.

Pay-per-click (PPC) – An advertising pricing model, also known as pay for performance, in which advertisers pay for their online ads based on how many consumers clicked on the ad. Two of the biggest online outlets for PPC advertising are Google AdWords and Microsoft Bing.

PayPal – A service that lets you take and make payments online; very handy as a method for the customer to pay for his purchase when using your shopping cart.

Paywall – A paywall is a website functionality restricting access to content, especially news, via a purchase or a paid subscription. Some paywalls allow access to a small portion of content before a pop-up blocks the rest of the content and explains that to see the rest of the content, you must pay for a subscription. Other paywalls show only the headline and none of the text.

PDF (Portable Document Format) – An electronic file format used to create and transmit documents with formatting, layout, and design. To view a PDF requires that the recipients have Adobe Acrobat Reader installed on their computers.

Penguin Theory – Penguin is an algorithm that automatically penalizes websites it sees as employing search engine optimization tactics deemed unacceptable by Google. The Penguin Theory is speculation about what actions and practices cause the Penguin algorithm to target your site. One bad practice that attracts the Penguin is having a large volume of inbound links to your site from low-quality sources. Also refers to any idea that looks good in black and white but just won't fly in the real world.

Periscope – A live streaming mobile app with 2 million users as of this writing.

Permission marketing – Advertising your product only to people who have agreed to allow you to do so; e.g., internet users who have signed up for a subscription to your digital newsletter, customers, association members.

Pinch point – Any factor that can cause the sales process to slow or derail; e.g., poor customer service, negative online reviews, shipping delays.[16]

PPC landing page – A web page designed to take clicks generated by PPC advertising and convert them into leads or sales. PPC landing pages are usually shorter and punchier than conventional landing pages. The reason is that the prospects clicking on your PPC ad don't know you and know almost nothing about your offer. Therefore, they are not as willing as, say, your newsletter subscribers, to read extremely long and involved copy. So, abbreviated landing pages convert PPC traffic better than conventional long-copy landing pages.

Pay-up – Getting customers who buy on a bill-me offer to pay for the product you sent them.

---

16   ANA Business Marketing SmartBrief, 8/4/2021.

PDF files – Adobe's portable document format (pdf) is a translation format used primarily for distributing files across a network or on a website. Files with a .pdf extension have been created in another application and then translated into .pdf files so they can be viewed by anyone, regardless of platform.

Penny saver – A free weekly newspaper serving the local community. These papers can be an effective and affordable advertising medium for contractors, restaurants, dentists, preschools, and other small businesses serving that community.

Perceived value – What a consumer believes a product is worth and is willing to pay for it.

Per diem – Fees charged by the day.

Per inquiry – Instead of paying a flat fee to run your ad, you pay the publication a percentage of every sale the ad produces or a dollar amount for every inquiry generated.

Permission marketing – Delivering marketing only to those consumers who have given you their permission to send it.

Personalization – Customizing a direct mail promotion or email marketing message with prospect data. The personalization can be superficial; e.g., just the recipient's name and address on the outer envelope and sales letter. Or it can be more extensive, depending on the data available for personalization. A mortgage mailer, for instance, might be personalized with the recipient's credit rating, current mortgage balance, and monthly mortgage payment. Generally, the more data you personalize a mailing with, the better the response, as long as the data is not inappropriate or too personal.

Photoshop – Software for manipulating photographs and other images on the computer.

Pica – 12-point type size; or a measurement of width with six picas to one inch.

Pins – Favorite links stored on Pinterest. Each pin is made up of a picture and a description given by the user. When you click on the link, the pin directs you to the image source page. Pins can be re-pinned by others.

Pinboard – Visual collection of pins organized by topic.

Pinterest – A social network where members post infographics and other visual contest to market their offers.

Pinterest board – A section of Pinterest you create for posting your graphics on a particular topic; you may have multiple boards, each on a different subject.

Pinterest pin – To take someone else's graphic and place it on one of your Pinterest boards. This is beneficial to the originator of the content as it gives his graphic broader exposure.

Pipeline – Leads from qualified prospects you are nurturing to turn them into paying clients. Also called a lead pipeline.

PI – Per inquiry advertising. Advertising for which the publisher or broadcast station is paid according to the number of inquiries produced by the ad or commercial.

Pitch slap – A negative comment or complaint about a post or comment you made on social media being too blatantly salesy or promotional.

Pivot – To quickly and nimbly change the direction of your marketing and business strategy in response to changing or uncertain marketplace conditions.

Pixel – The smallest unit or dot of a digitally displayed image.

Plug – A free mention, often a favorable comment or endorsement, given to a product by the media (e.g., TV and radio shows, newspapers, e-newsletters, website, etc.) without a charge to the product marketer or a fee to the show, publication, or website.

PMS (Pantone matching system) – A group of colors associated with a specific collection of inks.

Podcast – A non-streamed webcast in which a series of digital media files, most often mp3 audios, are released by the producer and often downloaded via an RSS feed.

Point-of-purchase (POP) display – A rack or other free-standing display used to promote products at the point of purchase; e.g., a self-standing cardboard display holding bags of a particular brand of potato chip, placed in a supermarket either at the end of an aisle or near the check-out line.

Polarization marketing – Taking a contrarian position on anything that's important to your market and the general public. People enjoy controversy and argument, and therefore, it gets their attention and effectively engages them. The portion of the market that agrees with your opinion, approach, technology, or methodology will pay more attention to you and become more likely to buy from you.

Poly bag – A clear bag used to hold and deliver promotional material or reading material, such as a magazine.

Pop-over – A page that pops up on the screen when you visit a website or landing page, the purpose of which is to capture the email address of the visitor, usually by offering free content.

Pop-under – A window that pops up on the screen when you attempt to leave a landing page or website without placing an order, the purpose of which is to capture the email address of the visitor, usually by offering free content.

Pop-up – A new window that suddenly appears on your computer screen when a web page is called up, and it frequently hides part of the content of the web page.

Portfolio – A presentation folder containing samples of your work. Shown to prospective employers when you are interviewing for a job.

Positioning – How your product compares with and is better than competing products in its category. Example: Schlitz beer "is the beer to have when you're having more than one" – a drinker's beer. Grey Poupon is positioned as a mustard for rich gourmets.

Post – For a consumer to leave a comment on a blog.

Postage meter – A machine that affixes to envelopes strips of paper that the post office accepts in lieu of postage stamps.

Postcard – A simple two-sided card sent through the mail.

Postcard deck – A deck of postcards, usually shrink-wrapped, with each card an advertisement for a different marketer.

Post office box (POB) – A box rented by a company or person so they can receive their mail at the post office rather than have it delivered to their office, plant, or house.

Predictive dialing – A system that dials consumers for telemarketing goals automatically. Whenever you pick up the phone and there is a pause of a few seconds before the telemarketer comes on the line, you know you were phoned by a predictive dialer.

Predictive research – Focus groups, interviews, and other market research techniques that attempt to predict which marketing approaches will work prior to testing them.

Preference form – A form the consumer fills out to let merchants he buys from know his purchase preferences. Preference forms for record clubs, for example, were used to ask consumers what type of music – country, classical, jazz, rock, easy listening – they liked best.

Premium – Free bonus gift offered to potential customers as motivation for buying a product or making an inquiry about a product.

Premium bandit – A customer who orders the product to get the free premium then returns the product for a refund while keeping the free gift.

Preprint – An insert in a newspaper from an advertiser that looks like a section of the newspaper and not like promotional material.

Press conference – Inviting reporters, journalists, and other bloggers to a briefing on some topic of interest, which in marketing, might be the introduction of the latest version of a popular technology product or the announcement of a new brand of automobile.

Presale page – A presale page, also called a doorway page, is a web page users see before arriving on your landing page. The presale page's objective is to help make potential customers want the product before they arrive at the landing page, where they can buy it online. Presale pages have usually have buttons hyperlinked to the landing page, so they can reach that page with a single click.

Press proof – The first piece off the press, used to check the color, quality, and appearance of the printed piece, before doing the entire press run.

Press release – Written news information distributed to the press, emailed to consumers, and posted on the marketer's website. The press release is intended to give journalists the idea to write a story about the marketer's company or products and the basic information to put in that story.

Primary colors – The colors that combine to form all other colors. In the CMYK system, they are cyan, magenta, and yellow; for the RGB system, red, green, and blue.

Prime Day – An annual promotion where Amazon makes special offers, good for one day only, to Amazon Prime members.

Primetime – Television broadcast between 8 pm and 11 pm EST.

Privacy policy – A statement explaining the steps you take to keep the customer's personal data private and confidential.

Private database – A database of prospects and customers you build and own for your company's use only.

Private label rights (PLR) – Digital products you can modify, reuse, or resell as you wish.

Probability tables – Statistical tables used to plan direct mail campaigns and determine what the likely response rate will be.

Product life cycle – The ups and downs in sales of a product over its lifetime. When you launch or introduce the product, you have no sales, and if your marketing is effective, you will build them. As the product gains a foothold in the marketplace and builds market share, there is sales growth. At some point, the product reaches the maturity phase, where other products and technologies are grabbing share away from it, and sales then start to fall in a period of decline. Eventually, sales and demand are so small that the marketer withdraws the product from the market, possibly replacing it with a different product or the next generation.

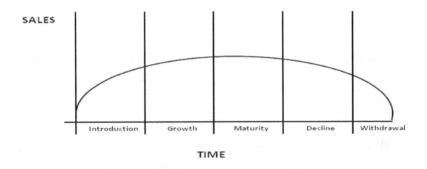

Product manager – A manager employed by an advertiser to supervise the marketing and advertising of a product or product line.

Product placement – Arranging to have your product features in a movie or TV show.

Product refund – A refund of the purchase price of a returned product minus the shipping and handling fee, which is not refunded.

Promotion – Activities other than advertising that are used to encourage the purchase of a product or service.

Profile – In social networks, a page telling others who you are, what you do, and what your work history and education are.

Profiling – Identifying demographics, firmographics, and lifestyle attributes of your ideal prospects and appending this information to the customer file.

Promo code – A code the consumer enters into a shopping cart page to get a discount on the product he or she is buying.

Proof – A single print of an original used to check the layout and color before the rest of the print run is produced on the press.

Programmatic marketing – Algorithms automating media buying and ad placement in online newsletters, magazines, social networks, and websites.

Prospect – A person with the money, authority, and desire to buy a product or service; a potential customer.

Prospecting – Marketing designed to generate inquiries about your product from potential customers. These promotions can include lead generation, social media, content marketing, and public speaking, to name just a few. The goal is to get new customers.

Proximity marketing – Marketing messages sent to consumers' mobile devices, triggered when the consumer is in close proximity to the marketer's place of business.

Proximity payment – Mobile payments made when both the customer and the merchant are in the same location, typically enabled through technologies including Near Field Communication (NFC), Quick Response (QR) codes, and Bluetooth.

Psychographics – Statistics relating to the personalities, attitudes, and lifestyles of various groups of people; e.g., religious beliefs, patriotism, political views, a preference for luxury cars, favorite alcoholic beverages.

Public database – A database that has identified names and addresses of consumers who use your product category but not necessarily your brand.

Pub-set – Ads designed and typeset by the publication in which they will appear.

Public service announcement (PSA) – A radio spot promoting a worthy cause for which the radio station does not charge the sponsor.

Public relations – The activity of influencing the press so that they print (and broadcast) stories that promote a favorable image of a company and its products.

Publisher's letter – See *Lift letter*.

Puffery – Exaggerated product claims made by an advertiser.

Pull – The response generated by an advertisement.

pURL (personalized URL) – In a marketing campaign, such as a postcard mailing, having a different URL for each recipient. This way, when prospects click on the URL in their postcard (or email or whatever marketing channel you are using), you know exactly who responded and what marketing piece they responded to.

Purpose-driven marketing – Aligning advertising, PR, and content around a social cause related to the company's core values.

Q

QR (Quick Response) code – A graphic imprinted on a print promotion such as a magazine ad or postcard; by running your smartphone over the QR code, you are immediately taken to a landing page or other web page related to the offer being promoted.

Quick-response bonus – A free gift given to consumers who respond quickly to an advertisement or promotion.

Qualified prospect – A person with the money, authority, and desire to buy your product, meaning they want it, can afford it, and are authorized to buy it.

Qualitative – Something that is measured subjectively and described in words but not numbered; e.g., participants in a focus group saying they like or don't like an ad.

Quantitative – Something that is measured precisely and can be expressed in numbers; e.g., a spectrophotometer measuring the color values of a package or product label.

Query – To look for a subject or item on a search engine by keyword.

Qwerty – Refers to a standard keyboard as they originated on typewriters and are used on most PCs today.

R

Radio button – A button on a landing page or website that allows the user to select only one item from a menu containing multiple options.

Rank – How high up a particular web page or site appears when users search on the related keyword. If you are not ranked high enough to show up on the first screen of the search engine results page (SERP), very few users will find your site on Google.

Rate buster – An advertiser who consistently negotiates with media to pay lower rates for advertising than what is listed on the publication's rate card.

Rate card – A sheet listing what it costs to advertise in a newspaper, magazine, or other publication.

Rating points – The percent of a total audience tuned in to a particular TV show.

Reach – The number of different people exposed to an advertising message within a specified period of time.

Reactivation – Marketing aimed at converting an inactive customer into an active customer by getting them to make a new purchase.

Recency – The date of the most recent purchase a customer has made.

Reciprocal link – An arrangement in which you link to someone's website and, in exchange, they link to yours.

Record – A single entry in a database for a single prospect containing all the information on that person that is available in the database. For instance, your record would contain your name, address, phone number, products purchased, dates of purchases, dollar amounts, and possibly a lot of other information such as age, gender, income, and occupation, to name just a few.

Red Book – Refers to both *The Standard Directory of Advertising Agencies* and *The Standard Directory of Advertisers*, directories of ad agencies and companies that advertise, respectively.

Reel – A reel of film or videotape containing sample commercials written by the copywriter.

Referral – When a customer or anyone else recommends you, your company, and your product or service to a friend, associate, or other person.

Referral marketing – Marketing aimed at generating referrals.

Referral rate – How frequently a merchant or vendor refers customers to other merchants or vendors; e.g., a dentist will refer children with crooked teeth to an orthodontist.

Reciprocal link – Two websites linking to each other. Reciprocal links enable the website owner to direct visitors to other websites they may find of interest. When you have reciprocal links to respected and highly rated websites, those reciprocal links can raise your site's search engine rankings.

Reciprocity – A principle that says if you do something for a prospect or customer (e.g., give them a free sample or free content), they will feel beholden to do something for you in return, such as read your ad and possibly buy your product.

Recurring revenue – Revenue produced through sales of a product or service on a weekly, monthly, or yearly basis; e.g., income properties generate monthly recurring revenue as rent payments made by tenants.

301 Redirect – A method of sending a user from one website or web page to another.

Reply elements – In a print ad or mailing, the form, response card, or coupon the consumer fills out and returns to request whatever was being offered in the promotion.

Repurpose – To take content created for one medium and reuse it in another; e.g., turning an article in your e-newsletter into a blog post. Also known as recycling.

RFM (recency, frequency, monetary) – Recency is the date of the consumer's last purchase; the more recent, the more likely the consumer is to respond to another promotion. Frequency is how often the consumer buys from you; the greater the frequency, the more likely they are to respond to the next promotion. Monetary refers to how much money on average they spend per order; the greater the monetary, the more likely they are to respond to higher-priced offers.

Regression analysis – A statistical process for analyzing the relationship between multiple variables in a marketing test or campaign to identify patterns that can lead to an increase in response.

Relational database – Files are placed into linked tables, as in a spreadsheet with rows and columns, and placed within a larger database structure. Data in tables is retrievable by category; e.g., you can pull all records of customers who are male, over 50, and have erectile dysfunction to sell them your testosterone boosting supplement.

Relationship marketing – Marketing that focuses on building relationships instead of making one-time sales.

Remnant space – Space for your ad a magazine sells you at a discount because nobody else bought it, and the magazine is about to go to press.

Renewal rate – The percentage of subscribers who renew their subscription in response to your renewal series (see below).

Renewal series – A sequence of letters and emails designed to get a subscriber of a publication or service to renew her subscription.

Reply card – A self-addressed postcard sent with advertising material to encourage the prospect to respond.

Reply Rate – The percentage of people receiving your direct mail or email who respond to it.

Reprint – Copies of a feature article to be used as mailers or sales literature by the marketer whose company or product is featured in the article.

Research – Surveys, interviews, and studies designed to show an advertiser how the public perceives his product and company or how they react to the advertiser's ads and commercials.

Response list – A mailing list of people who have in the past purchased something in response to a direct mailing, advertisement, or other promotion. Response lists usually get better responses than compiled lists. The reason is that not everyone buys from direct marketing offers, but everyone on a response list has.

Response rate –The percentage of people receiving or seeing a promotion who respond to it. If you send out a thousand sales letters and get 20 orders, your response rate is 2 percent.

Reseller – A company that sells products made by other companies.

Retargeting – Showing users who viewed an ad on a website the exact same ad on other websites he or she visits. For instance, when advertising on Facebook, you supply Facebook with a listing of your customers and prospects with names and email addresses. Facebook algorithms identify other FB users who are good prospects based on their extensive data on Facebook users. Your Facebook ad is targeted not only to your customers and prospects but also "retargeted" to FB users whose characteristics are similar to your customers' demographics and psychographics. For example, if your e-list is mostly optical engineers, Facebook will identify Facebook users who are also optical engineers and serve them your ad through retargeting.

Retention – Keeping a customer as an active customer. The retention rate is the percentage of your customers who continue to do business with you in a given time period, usually 12 months, but can vary with industry.

Return on investment (ROI) – The amount of money you make in sales compared with the amount of money you spend on marketing. If you make $2 for every $1 spent on advertising, your ROI is 100 percent or 2:1.

Reverse type – White type on a black background.

Rewards program – The consumer is awarded points based on the amount of money she spends with the merchant. The points can be redeemed for merchandise, travel, or other free gifts.

RGB color – In computer screens and other electronic devices, all colors are produced by mixing three basic colors: red, green, and blue.

Rich media – Online ads or emails that contain changing images, streaming videos, or applets.

Right-brain advertising – Ads that appeal primarily to emotion.

Risk-free offer – Where the product is sold on an unconditional money-back guarantee basis. That is, if you don't like it, you may return it within a specified time period for a full refund.

Roll-out – To ramp up a marketing campaign and mail to more people on a mailing list following a successful test on a smaller scale. For instance, if you mail 5,000 direct mail pieces and get a good response, you roll out and with confidence, mail another 25,000 to 50,000 or so.

Roll-out rule – The roll-out rule says that after a successful direct mail test, you can safely roll out to up to ten times the size of the test cell. So, if you tested 5,000 names, you could roll out that same mailer to up to 50,000 names on that same list.

ROP (run of paper) – Ads that the advertiser allows the newspaper to run anywhere in the paper instead of in a specific section like sports or local news.

Rotating banner – When the top portion of your home page cycles between multiple versions. The idea is to appeal to multiple audiences or highlight multiple features or advantages. But studies have shown that rotating banners are less effective than static banners. One problem with rotating banners is that, just as you are reading it, the copy rotates away and is replaced by another message.

RSS (Really Simple Syndication) – A family of web feeds that allow you to receive or distribute information without having to constantly open new pages in your browser. Content publishers can syndicate a feed, which allows users to subscribe to the content and read it when they please from a location other than the website.

Run of network – A media buy in which the network owner has the option of placing the ad on any page on any website within that ad network.

Run of site – A media buy-in which a website owner has the option of placing the ad on any page within the website.

Run of press/run of paper – When the publisher can place your ad anywhere in the newspaper or magazine where he has space vs. a preferred position like the inside front cover of a magazine or the front page of the gardening section of the paper.

Run of schedule – A commercial that can be run any time of the day or night.

Run time – The length of a video.

S

S-pattern – A theory that when people read a newspaper, they scan the pages in an S pattern, starting at the top right corner and following the shape of an S.

Saas – "Software as a service" means you subscribe to the software and access it over the internet vs. traditional software that you buy or license rather than subscribe to and get as a download or (very rarely these days) mailed to you on a CD.

Saddle stitch – To bind pages by stapling a publication from the back spine to the center.

Sales appeal – The reasons why consumers would want to buy the product; e.g., to look better, to lose weight, to save time or money, etc.

Sales cycle – The steps the consumer goes through to reach a decision about purchasing the product.

Sales lead – An inquiry from a qualified prospect.

Sales-enablement content – Content used by the sales team to help them make a sale or by the prospect to make a purchase decision.[17]

Sales funnel – A series of marketing efforts designed to first turn a prospect into a customer and then get the customer to buy increasingly more expensive products and services. At the top of the funnel, the first step is to get prospects to enter into the funnel. This is accomplished using any of a number of marketing techniques (e.g., email, ads) with a call-to-action (CTA). The CTA typically gets a lead to opt-in to your email list by offering free content. Once we get prospects to enter our funnel, we move them through a sequence of steps down the funnel. At the bottom of the funnel, we convert qualified prospects to customers by getting them to place their first order with us.

Sales pitch – The presentation of arguments or reasons made by a salesperson or ad to convince the consumer to buy the product.

---

17   Content Marketing Institute, 7/29/2021.

Sales promotion – A temporary marketing effort designed to generate short-term interest in the purchase of a product. Coupons, sales, discounts, premiums, sweepstakes, and contests are all examples of sales promotion.

Sales sheet – An 8 ½ by 11-inch sheet of paper with copy and artwork designed to sell a product. Can also be in PDF format.

Sampling – Distributing free samples of your product to potential customers.

Sans serif – Type without little lines extending from the letters. Arial is a sans serif type.

SCF (sectional center) – Postal Service distribution unit made up of different post offices whose zip codes start with the first three digits.

Scratch-and-sniff – A piece of card stock or paper impregnated with a perfume, fragrance, or other odor, which is released and intensified when the surface is scratched. In one industrial mailing, our scratch-and-sniff smelled like rotten eggs to help the prospect become familiar with the odor of a gas leak.

Scratch-off – A reply device or card that the consumer has to scratch to reveal whether he has won a prize. Also used in lottery tickets. You rub a portion of the card with the edge of a coin to reveal the words underneath.

Search engine – Google, Yahoo, Bing, and other algorithms that search the internet for information by keyword.

Search engine optimization (SEO) – A group of website copywriting and design practices aimed at making a website come up higher in the search engine rankings when keywords important to the website owner and his customers are searched. For instance, one such technique is to use the keyword phrase frequently in your home page copy. Another SEO technique is to have a large amount of keyword-rich content on your site. A third is to have many links from recognized sites in your niche going to your site.

Search engine results page (SERP) – The page displaying the sites that come up as a result of a keyword search.

Seed – Putting fake names in a mailing list. Why? Mailing lists are generally rented for one-time usage. The seed name is really an address or PO box used by the list owner. If the mailer cheats and uses the list twice, the owner gets the mail piece at the seed address twice and knows that the mailer has violated the terms of the agreement – in other words, has cheated.

Segmentation – Separating names on a list by demographics and psychographics, so you can select names on the list by these characteristics for targeted marketing efforts; e.g., if you have a list of high school students, you may treat each grade as a separate segment, and then do a mailing offering a class ring to seniors only.

Segmentation analysis – Measuring and analyzing marketing campaign performance by market segments. For instance, in a campaign aimed at doctors, you may find that neurosurgeons spend more and respond better than anesthesiologists.

Segmented editions – Editions of a newspaper or magazine targeted to specific regions or states. Advertising in a segmented edition targeting just your geographic market is much less expensive than advertising to the full national circulation of that publication.

Select – A demographic, psychographic, or other variable by which you can select which names on a mailing list you want to mail to. For instance, on a business list, you can choose to rent the names of only those companies with 100 or more employees or at least $10 million in sales.

Self-mailer – A direct mail promotion that is mailed without an outer envelope.

Sell sheet – A piece of promotional literature with copy and graphics on two sides of an 8 ½ by 11-inch piece of paper or PDF; also called a flier or, when advertising technical products, a datasheet.

Separations – In four-color printing, a separate overlay is used for each color or achieved photographically by using filters.

Serial returners – Customers who repeatedly buy products that they quickly return after using them once, such as a pair of expensive shoes "borrowed" in this questionable matter for a wedding or other special occasion.

Search engine – An algorithm that can find information on the internet by keyword.

SEM (search engine marketing) – Marketing tactics and campaigns where search engines are an integral part of the promotion.

SEO (search engine optimization) – A procedure for getting your website to rank higher in the search engines, so that when someone searches your keywords, they are more likely to come up with your company on the search engine results page.

SERP (Search engine results page) – The portion of the screen where the results of your search show up on a search engine. The goal of search engine optimization is to have your company show up on the first SERP screen when people search your keyword. The SERP shows the URLs, titles, and descriptions of websites found by search engines in response to a user searching a specific keyword or keyword phrase.

Self-mailer – Direct mail promotion mailed without an envelope, typically a folded sheet of paper.

Selling – Communicating with a person face-to-face or over the phone for purposes of persuading them to buy your product.

Serif type – Type with little lines called serifs extending from the letter. Times Roman is a serif type.

Session – The length of time a user spends on a particular website.

SIC (Standard Industrial Code) – An older, mostly outdated system that uses a 4-digit code for identifying industries.

Shareable – Content that can be transmitted or shared by a third party; e.g., you clip a paragraph from my blog and post it on your Facebook page.

Shipping and handling – The cost of getting the product to the customer. Calculated by adding postage or shipping charges to the fulfillment or handling charge. For instance, if the shipping charge is $10 and your fulfillment operation charges $2 to pack and ship the item, your shipping and handling charge is $12. Most often, merchants add the shipping and handling charge to the cost of the product when selling merchandise. So, for a $70 product with $12 shipping and handling, you would pay $82.

Shock and awe package – A type of "inquiry fulfillment package" (see definition). A big package of lots of stuff that is sent to people who want more information about your product or service. The shock and awe package is typically mailed in a large padded envelope or a box. Items in the shock and awe package can include a cover letter, product literature, a book, audio CDs, DVDs, and "ad specialties" (see definition) such as pens, mini-flashlights, sticky note pads, a coffee mug, candy – you name it. The contents are referred to as swag, and the shock and awe package is sometimes called a swag box.

Shook – A short book, usually less than 100 pages, written specifically as a marketing tool. Shooks can be premiums given with purchase; quick-response bonuses that give the customer an added reason to buy a product now instead of later; a reward to loyal customers; a value-added component of a product (e.g., a companion book given with an exercise DVD or ab machine); a reward for referrals; a welcome gift to new members or subscribers.

Shoppable content – Online copy and images of a product that you can not only view and read about but actually purchase online while viewing the content, just by clicking on the image, a button, or other hyperlink to a sales page or e-commerce site.

Shopping cart – Software that enables your website with e-commerce so your customers can buy your products from you online. Examples include the popular software Infusionsoft and 1shoppingcart.

Showrooming – When customers come into a store, look at the merchandise, check the prices, and then buy the product online for a lower price. Can also happen with print catalogs.

Silk screen – To imprint a surface with a graphic image by forcing ink through a stencil placed over a screen.

Site map – A web page that displays an outline of the pages on your site, showing what they are and how they are organized; having a site map can improve your search engine rankings.

Site retargeting – You place a cookie in the browser of a visitor to your site. Now, your ad can be displayed again when the user visits another site in the ad network.

Sidebar – A short section of copy separated from the main text by a box or border.

Signage – Signs advertising a product or offer put in the windows of stores and elsewhere, usually highlighting a sale.

Silk screen – A printing method in which ink is forced through a stencil placed over a screen. The ink passes through the screen onto a substrate, except where it is blocked by the stencil. The substrate is the material the printing appears on. Silk screen is often applied to plastic signs and trade show displays, posters, and T-shirts.

Site map – An XML file or directory listing the pages on your website, including the schemata in which they are organized and linked.

Sketch video – A video in which, while the narrator speaks, the screen shows a cartoon hand or pencil sketching the accompanying visuals. These are usually, but not always, fairly simple drawings or sketches. Also known as a whiteboard video.

Skyrocket – A sharp upswing in sales, response rates, or other marketing results.

Skyscraper – A tall, thin banner ad shaped like a skyscraper.

SlideShare – An online social network for sharing your PowerPoint presentations.

Slim jim – A small brochure printed on a letter or legal-size sheet of paper folded down to fit a number ten outer envelope or fit in a brochure display rack typically found in a bank or travel agency; usually has four, six, or eight pages.

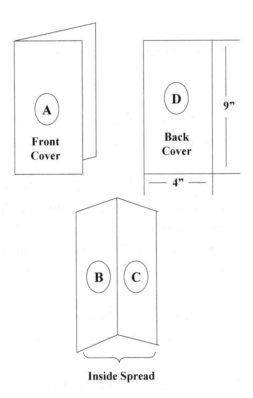

Inside Spread

Slogan – A short line of copy that sums up the brand's positioning and appears in most of its advertising; e.g., Maxwell House: Good to the Last Drop. In print, also known as a tag line.

Slug – Letters or words added to a website URL after the .com that direct the browser to a particular page. For instance, www.bly.com links to the home page of my website. When you add "reports" as a slug, www.bly.com/reports takes you to the subscription page for my free online newsletter, The Direct Response Letter. The hosting charge for the main site also covered slug pages. So, slugs allow you to have unique URLs without registering a whole new domain name or paying an additional fee to host the slug URL.

Splash page – An image, decorative, or branding page visitors see first and must pass through to get to the website home page. Once common, splash pages have fallen out of favor.

Spider – Also known as bots, spiders are automated programs that visit web pages to help determine their ranking on the search engines.

Snapchat – A social media network where users can take "Snaps" – photos, video, text, drawings – and send them to a list. The Snaps can be viewed for a few seconds before they are deleted from Snapchat's servers. Billions of videos and photos are sent on Snapchat daily.

Snap pack – A direct mail format consisting of multiple plies or sheets of thin paper, with a border you must tear off to separate and read the plies. The border of a snap pack is usually imprinted with text, such as "Tear off to open." Some companies send invoices or checks as snap packs.

Spiff – Gifts in the medium to medium/high-end price range in value but given free to good customers who spend significant amounts of money on your products and services.

Split testing – Running two different versions of an ad, email, or mailing to see which generates the greater response.

Spot color – Enhancing a black and white advertisement with a second color applied sparingly.

Social media – A network on the internet where people can communicate with one another and share content; e.g., Facebook, Twitter, LinkedIn, Google+.

Social media marketing – Actively and purposefully using social media to market your product or service.

Social networking – Posting and commenting on social media; e.g., posting something on Facebook and responding to the comments you get.

Social proof – Convincing the market your product or service must be good because other people like it. Examples include online reviews, brisk demand, fan clubs, enthusiasts, huge membership, and a best-selling product.

Soft bounce – Email not delivered for reasons other than a bad address; e.g., the text contains words that cause the email to be blocked by spam filters.

Soft offer – An offer in which the consumer does not have to pay upfront. The product is sent on a bill-me basis, meaning the consumer will receive an invoice for what he has ordered.

Software-as-a-Service (SaaS) – Applications and other software that you may license and use but are stored on the seller's service, not yours. Example: 1shoppingcart.

SOHO (small office/home office) – A small business with just a few employees; often run out of the owner's home.

Solo ad – An ad in an online newsletter that is the only advertisement in that particular issue.

Solo mailing – One mailing offering one product.

Space – The portion of a magazine or newspaper devoted to advertisements.

Space ads – Ads appearing in newspapers and magazines.

Spam – Sending promotional emails to people who have not opted in to your e-list and therefore have not agreed to get advertising emails from you; sending consumers emails they do not want and perceive as junk.

Speculative presentation – An ad campaign created by an ad agency with no compensation in the hopes of winning business from that particular advertiser.

Special report – Free content offered as an incentive for the visitor to take action, typically either placing an order or giving you his email address; very similar to a white paper.

Splash page – An eye-catching web page with attractive graphics that appears before the site's home page. Splash pages have fallen out of favor.

Spelling Nazi – A consumer obsessed with pointing out typos in marketing materials to the marketers.

Split run test – Two versions of an ad are run in different copies of a publication to test the effectiveness of one version against the other.

Split tests can be done in almost any media generating a measurable response. For instance, you can split test two online ads, two postcards, and so on. (See also *A/B split*.)

Spokesperson – An actor or celebrity who regularly appears in TV commercials and ads for a given product; e.g., Shaq is the spokesperson for Icy Hot; George Foreman for the George Foreman Grill.

Sponsored content – Advertising on a media outlet in the guise of editorial content (articles) that looks like it's supposed to be there; very similar to native advertising.

Spread – An article or ad that goes across two pages, the left and the right facing it. The horizontal line between the two pages in a spread is called the gutter.

Square inch analysis – In a catalog, you divide the total sales for a given product by the square inches of space dedicated to that item in the catalog to get the sales per square inch. This way, you can compare the relative performance of different items in the catalog.

Squeeze Pages – See *Name squeeze page*.

Standard Industrial Code (SIC) – Codes that classify companies by the industry they are in.

Statistically valid – Knowing a marketing test or survey was conducted with a large enough audience so you can rely on and trust in the results.

Standard Rate and Data Service (SRDS) – Media directories covering mailing lists and magazines, provided to data marketers who need to decide whether to rent a list or advertising in a publication.

Stickiness – How long a time visitors spend on your website.

Stock photography – A collection of existing photos you can license to use in your marketing materials or other publications.

Storyboards – A series of rough sketches that outline the shots in a planned TV commercial in sequence.

Strategic planning – Coordinating an orchestrated campaign of multiple marketing tactics and channels to achieve a specific marketing objective.

Story – Making the case for why consumers should buy your product with an ad written as a story.

Storyboard – Rough series of illustrations showing what a finished TV commercial will look like.

Story-driven marketing – Marketing in which the copy is written as a story rather than traditional sales copy. The idea is that stories capture human attention and interest more so than straightforward product description or sales copy.

Stuffers – Printed promotional pieces inserted in mailings for other products as well as other media.

Supply Side Platform (SSP) – A software platform that connects publishers and other websites that accept advertising with advertisers who might like to run ads in that digital publication or site.

Sturgeon's Law – The principle that 90 percent of everything – advertisements, websites, social media, pizzas, cars, microwave ovens – is of inferior quality.

Subhead – A second headline in smaller type under the main headline but before the main text of an ad, letter, or web page. Or a line of boldface type used to break up long body copy, usually centered.

Subjective judgment – Making marketing decisions based on personal opinion and preferences rather than facts and testing. For instance, a young marketer recently told me that advertising on AM radio is old-fashioned, and no one listens to radio anymore. Yet global annual advertising expenditures for radio are about $34 billion.

Subliminal advertising – Advertising that somehow targets your subconscious mind. Example: a TV commercial that embeds images shown so quickly they don't register in your conscious mind.

Subscriber – In internet marketing, someone who has opted into your e-list to receive your online newsletter.

Super affiliates – The one percent of your affiliates generating 99 percent of your affiliate sales. These are large and successful internet marketers with big and responsive lists who can move a lot of your product. For instance, one of my super affiliates sold almost 1,000 copies of one of my e-books with a single email blast to their list.

Supermarket pricing – Prices with numbers to the right of the decimal; e.g., $9.99 vs. $10.

Suppression – To deliberately not mail to certain people on a list for a variety of reasons; e.g., they are known to be deadbeats; their credit scores are low.

Survey monkey – Surveymonkey.com is software that enables you to conduct surveys quickly and affordably online.

Suspect – Someone who responds to an ad but has not yet been confirmed to be a qualified prospect with the money, authority, and desire to buy your product.

Sweepstakes – A sales promotion in which prizes are awarded by chance and the consumer does not have to make a purchase to enter.

Swipe file – A file of ads you collect for reference, inspiration, ideas, or to emulate.

SWOT – A method of analyzing competitors based on strengths, weaknesses, opportunities, and threats.

T

Tabloid – An oversize self-mailer with the same dimensions as a tabloid newspaper; or a newspaper that publishes sensationalist journalism of questionable integrity.

Tag line – A slogan.

Taguchi Testing – Also known as multivariate testing software that enables you to test many elements on a landing page – including headline, visual, offer, placement of reply element, copy, and video – at once. Taguchi software enables multiple variables with multiple versions to be tested simultaneously, unlike traditional A/B testing that tests only two versions of one parameter; e.g., envelope teaser vs. no teaser.

Takeaway close – A sales technique in which you cause the prospect to want to buy by telling him he cannot have the product or by making it difficult to get.

Target market – The specific group of consumers a marketing campaign is aimed at.

Targeting – Aiming your marketing efforts at a specific group of buyers; e.g., chiropractors, men over 60.

Tear-off stub – A small portion of a business reply card, coupon, ticket, or other paper promotion separated from the main portion by a vertical perforation, so the stub can be easily separated. In a business reply card, the main portion is mailed back to the advertiser, while the stub is used as a receipt or record of the transaction.

Tear sheet mailer – A direct mail piece resembling an article torn out of a magazine or newspaper and inserted into an envelope, sometimes with a Post-It note attached.

Teaser – Copy printed on the outside envelope of a direct mail package.

Teleseminar – A seminar or talk given to multiple listeners by a presenter over a bridge or conference line.

Test – To test one or more variations or variables in a marketing campaign to see which produces better results.

Testimonial – A statement from a customer praising your company or your product or service.

Tests and continuations – Tests refer to the number of marketers who have tested the list, and continuations refers to those marketers who, after a test, come back to rent more names on the list. If the percentage of continuations is 7 out of 10 or higher, that's an indication that the list is working.

Text ad – An ad in an online newsletter that is all text and contains no images, but there is a link to a landing page where the prospect can get more information about the offer or place an order.

Text email – An email that uses text and straight type only, no HTML or images.

Third-party logistics (3PL) – Outsourcing by retailers and brands of fulfillment, pickup, returns, and other logistics to outside service providers such as UPS, DHL, and FedEx.

Three-martini lunch – A long lunch in an expensive restaurant that ad agency personnel treat their clients to. Once commonplace, it is now fading away as people are too busy for it.

Thumb drive collateral – A USB stick on which multiple marketing materials are stored as digital files, which prospects can access and download on their devices. The USB sticks may be handed to prospects by salespeople, given away at trade shows, or delivered via postal mail.

Thumbnail – A small, rough sketch to show the proposed layout of an ad.

TIFF (Tagged Image File Format) – An image file format that contains information on the brightness and hue of every pixel.

Till forbid – A continuity program that continues to send and bill you for products until you tell them to stop. Also called a negative option.

Tip sheet – An 8 ½ by 11-inch page with tips relating to a particular topic on one or both sides.

Tipographic – A slim vertical box with some tips on a specific topic that is posted on Pinterest and Instagram.

Tire-kicker – A consumer who wastes marketers' time with endless questions about the product but never, ever buys anything.

Token – A sticker or other removable device that the consumer may add to the order form to indicate acceptance of the offer.

Tomfoolery – Jokes or pranks perpetrated on the public by marketers; e.g., Proctor & Gamble announcing that it was introducing bacon-flavored mouthwash.

Top-level domain (TLD) – The suffix of the domain name; e.g., the TLD of www.art.org is .org.

Top-level web page – A web page accessible by clicking on a button in the menu on the home page.

Top of the funnel – Efforts to attract potential prospects to interact with the brand at the earliest level of lead generation and the sales process.

15 Tips

for Profitable PDF E-Book Publishing

1. Use an 8 ½ X 11-inch page size.
2. Aim for 50 pages – around 15,000 words.
3. Create a landing page to sell the e-book. Example: www.myveryfirstebook.com
4. Write as an expert, not a journalist.
5. Don't just collect and rewrite articles from Google.
6. Interview subject matter experts.
7. Participate in the skill or activity you write about.
8. Pack your book with practical tips.
9. Give step-by-step how-to instruction.
10. Use real-life examples.
11. Don't give a lot of theory or background.
12. Write in simple and straightforward prose.
13. Give away a free bonus report with purchase.
14. Offer a 90-day money-back guarantee.
15. Price the e-book between $19 and $49.

For more tips on e-book profits:
www.myveryfirstebook.com

Total Addressable Market (TAM) – The portion of the total universe of potential buyers that you can reach through one or more marketing channels. A prospect with no internet access, for example, would still be part of the TAM, assuming he listened to the radio, because you could reach him through radio ads.

Touch – To reach or connect with a consumer through one of your promotions.

Toyetic – The suitability of a media property, such as a cartoon or movie, for merchandising tie-in lines of licensed toys, games, and novelties.

Tracking – Using key codes, pURLs, cookies, and other methods to track where responses to your ad campaign came from and how well each marketing tactic is performing.

Tracking pixel – A small piece of HTML code that is loaded when a user visits a website or opens an email. It is used to track user behavior and conversions.

Trade advertising – Advertising aimed at wholesalers, distributors, sales reps, agents, and retailers rather than consumers.

Trade journal – A business magazine covering a specific industry or vertical niche.

Trade promotion – Marketing targeted to dealers, distributors, and stores to get them to carry your line of products and sell it aggressively.

Trade show – An exhibition by multiple advertisers. Each advertiser has a booth promoting its products. These display booths have pictures of the products on the walls of the booth. Actual products – or for large ones, models of projects – may also be shown.

Trademark – (1) A logo or other symbol used in trade to identify a company or product. (2) A form of limited legal protection that prevents other companies from copying your slogan or product names.

Traffic – The number of visitors to a website or other location on the web, typically measured by them clicking onto one of your web pages.

Traffic manager – Employee at an ad agency responsible for making sure all client projects are completed to specification and on time.

Traffic, paid – Traffic driven to a website through any kind of paid advertising such as Google ads and Facebook ads.

Transaction page – An order page.

Transactional email – An email sent because a specific transaction has taken place; e.g., you send an email to everyone on your list who has bought bird seed in the last 12 months, offering them a birdhouse.

Transit advertising – Ads on buses, trains, and subways; also in bus and train stations.

Trial – In a risk-free trial, also called a no-risk trial, the product is purchased on a conditional basis, where if the customer is not happy, he has a certain amount of time to return the product for a refund. In comparison, a *free trial* means the customer is sent the product to try without paying for it. If she likes the product, she keeps and pays for it. If she does not like it, she returns the product and pays nothing. In a risk-free trial, you can ask for the customer's credit card information. But in a free trial, you cannot because when you ask for the credit card before you ship the product, customers perceive the offer as not free, and your advertising was dishonest. Even if you take the credit card number but promise not to charge it until the trial period is over and the customer decides to buy, many consumers think that if the trial was truly free, the merchant would not need the credit card number.

Trifold – A self-mailer or small brochure made by folding an 8 ½ by 11-inch sheet of paper twice horizontally so it can fit in a rack or #10 envelope.

Trigger email – An email that is sent when a specific action takes place; e.g., when a prospect downloads a white paper, completes an online survey, or makes a purchase.

Trim size – The desired size of a printed document, made by trimming or cutting the pages to the precise dimensions required.

Tripwire marketing – Turning a lead into a customer by offering them a low-priced product, then, once you get them into your sales funnel, upselling them to more expensive products.

Twitter – A social network that allows users to send messages or "tweets" of up to 140 characters.

Two color – An ad or sales brochure printed in two colors, usually black and a second color such as blue, red, or yellow.

Two-step promotion – Marketing that generates a lead, which is then followed up to close the sale. Example: a TV commercial for reverse mortgages offering a free information kit. When you call to get the kit, a salesperson either then or later tries to get you to take the reverse mortgage.

Type – Text set in lettering that can be reproduced by a printer.

Typeface – The design of the lettering. This typeface is Garamond. This type is Calibri.

U

Unattributed testimonial – Putting quotation marks around text to make it look like a testimonial when in fact, it is not.

Uncoated paper – Paper without an additional protective coating of varnish.

Unconditional guarantee – This means a refund is given no matter what – no ifs, ands, or buts. Customer ripped up the box? Product has wear and tear? He still gets the refund.

Ungated content – Free content the prospect can view and download without having to give any personal information or fill out a form. The reason some marketers offer ungated vs. gated content is that ungated content gets many more downloads. But gated content captures leads and adds new names to your e-list.

User experience – The experience users have when researching product information, purchasing products online, accessing online tools and content, and finding what they are looking for on your site.

User-generated content (UGC) – Content posted on your website by customers, prospects, product reviewers, and other site visitors vs. content you create and post.

UGC, shoppable – User-generated content that facilitates online purchasing because it's only one or two clicks away from getting to the product order page or sales page. Nearly 8 out of 10 people say UGC highly impacts their purchasing decisions, and 7 out of 10 trust user-generated content more than branded content.[18]

Unique visitor – Each person who has visited your website is a unique visitor. If Dick clicks onto your site five times and Janes clicks onto it one, you have six hits but only two unique visitors, Dick and Jane.

Unique selling proposition (USP) – The feature, benefit, or other advantage that makes your product different and better than your competitors' product. The USP can be the popularity of the brand (e.g., Coca-Cola) or superiority of design or function (e.g., Apple computers). The concept was most famously articulated by Rosser Reeves in his book *Reality in Advertising.* He notes the USP has to be a significant benefit that other products do not have, not a minor point of difference – so powerful that it can motivate large numbers of consumers to try the product.

Universe – The total number of people who are prospects for your product.

Upscale – Prospects at the upper end of the social scale in terms of income, education, and status.

---

18 Social Media Today, "Why Shoppable UGC is the Future of eCommerce Experiences," Peter Cassidy, 4/25/21.

Upsell – When the customer orders the product, offering her either a deluxe model at a higher price, an extended warranty service plan, optional attachments, or other items that will increase the total purchase price if she accepts the offer.

UPS – United Parcel Service, a commercial package delivery service.

Unsubscribe – To ask the publisher of an e-newsletter or the owner of an opt-in email list to remove your name from their list. Every time you email the list, some people will unsubscribe. Your unsubscribe rate ideally should be no more than 0.1 percent per email.

Urgency – Refers to the need of some consumers to buy now instead of later; e.g., a person shopping for a new air conditioner when the temperature outside is 90 degrees F feels some urgency about buying and installing a new unit right away.

URL – A unique website domain name (uniform resource locator) such as www.buildyourlistfast.net.

Usenet – A global, distributed discussion system available to users of computers and mobile devices.

UGC (user-generated content) – Content that has been created and published online by the users of a social network or collaboration platform, typically for non-commercial purposes. Every time you post to Facebook, you have posted UGC.

URL shortener – An online tool that condenses a long URL into a shorter one, so it is less awkward and more memorable. Users who click on the shortened URL are redirected to the original URL.

Usability – How easy it is for users to navigate a website and find the information they are looking for.

Usability testing – Tests designed to measure the usability of a website.

User-centered design – A website or page designed for ease of use, viewing, and reading.

User interface – The design and functionality of the screen the user is viewing and using.

User-generated content – Content produced by a user instead of a marketer. Examples include comments on blogs, homemade YouTube videos, and online product reviews.

User-research – Understanding user behaviors, needs, and motivations through observation techniques, task analysis, and other feedback methodologies.

USPS – United States Postal Services.

UX – (1) A collection of myths, misconceptions, and falsehoods about marketing that, in fact, are not true. (2) An abbreviation for "user experience," which is the total experience of visiting your website; e.g., watching the videos, downloading the white papers, reading the FAQs, making an online purchase. UX copywriting is valuable in that it improves the user experience, which in turn can increase conversion of visitors to leads up to fivefold.[19]

---

19 Callum Dunbar, Future Content, "UX Copywriting: What is it and why does it matter."

V

VALS (values and lifestyles) – A method of classifying people by their values and identifying their geographic distribution by neighborhoods; used to find prospects.

Value added – An optional feature or extra service bundled with a product to make it more useful and valuable to the consumer. An example is cars the dealer has equipped with built-in navigation and emergency help systems; the benefit is you never get lost or stranded roadside.

Value-added service – A service offered by a merchant that enables them to compete with lower-priced competitors. Example: Best Buy supports the electronics it sells with the Geek Squad troubleshooting and repair service.

Value proposition – The benefits, usage, prestige, or other value the customer gets when she purchases your product; the one big compelling reason why the consumer would desire and buy your product..

Vanity metrics – Data, measurements, and analytics that serve no purpose and do not help improve marketing.

Variable date printing – A type of digital printing that allows you to personalize mailings by printing people's names or other text on each piece, or changing out photos or graphics, without stopping or slowing down the printing process. You can also print variable QR codes, PURLs or barcodes. This allows you to present a very targeted, individualized message even though you're doing a mass mailing.

Vellum – A strong, thick glossy paper. Often placed in books or brochures for a distinctive look.

Version – A variation of a promotion with some alterations from the original. Different versions are often tested against one another to see which pulls the most response.

Vertical market – A narrow and specialized market; e.g., endodontists, coin collectors, sailors.

Vertical publication – A magazine or newsletter intended for a narrow group of people with shared special interests or in a specific profession or industry.

Video matching – Having a machine read barcodes on mail pieces to make sure the elements and the envelope are matched correctly.

Video, online – Refers most often to videos posted on the home page or other pages of websites. Vidyard and Demand Metric report[20] that about 60 percent of videos created by businesses are less than 2 minutes long. Some 58 percent of viewers, on average, finish watching videos less than 1 minute long. And about 24 percent will watch to completion videos with run times over 20 minutes.

---

20   https://www.marketingprofs.com/charts/2021/44797/business-video-benchmarks-content-engagement-and-distribution-trends

Video, personalized – Marketing videos that are personalized with data specific to each individual viewing the video; e.g., videos that show the recipient's name on the screen using text-field inserts and overlays.[21]

Video sales letter (VSL) – Instead of posting a sales letter on the web, the marketer posts a video in which the copy is spoken by a narrator. The visuals are usually sketched as the narrator talks (see *Sketch videos*), though in the early days of video sales letters, all that appeared on the screen was PowerPoint slides with the words of the script on them.

Vital content – Content that is either so informative, useful, or entertaining that people proactively pass it on to their friends and colleagues.

Viral marketing – Marketing so clever, entertaining, enticing, or informative that consumers forward it to their friends and acquaintances. Some marketers set out to deliberately make their campaigns viral, while for others, it just happens.

Visitor – A person who clicks onto your website or page.

Voice over – A TV or radio commercial or movie trailer read by an announcer who is not on screen.

Voucher – A direct mail format that is a cross between an invoice, an order form, and a sales flier.

---

21   Content Marketing Institute, 8/5/2021.

W

WAP (wireless application protocol) – A set of standards that allows web access on mobile devices.

Watermark – Designs on sheets of paper created by various paper thicknesses. They are often used on stationery to add a look of elegance or importance.

Web 1.0 – The web years ago when it consisted mainly of static pages and websites without much interactivity.

Web 2.0 – The web of today where social media sites and functionality built into websites give users a higher level of interactivity.

Webinar – A presentation or seminar given to multiple attendees over the web and phone lines. Also known as a webcast.

Web page – A single page on a website.

Web page, first level – A page on a major topic reachable by clicking a button on the home page.

Web page, second level – A page on a secondary topic reachable by clicking a hyperlink on a first-level page.

Website – A connected group of HTML web pages found at a single URL address and working as a whole to provide complete information on a company and its products.

Whiteboard – Any online video where drawings or text appear on a white background as the narration unfolds. The text slides are usually made using PowerPoint or sketches.

White Hat SEO – Legitimate search engine optimization techniques approved of by the major search engines.

White mail – Letters sent by a consumer to the advertiser that contain a communication other than an order.

White paper – A marketing communication that combines the characteristics of an article or informational report and a sales brochure. Its aim is to educate the consumer in a way that makes him more predisposed to buy the product being promoted. It typically focuses on the problem the product solves, the methodology of the marketer's service, or the technology of the marketer's product.

White space – Empty space on a page or screen containing no text or images. Some graphic designers see white space as a design element that makes pages and screens easier to read and less intimidating; many direct marketers think white space is a waste of space.

Widget – A small piece of software, usually on the web, that performs some useful function for your prospect.

Wiki – A site that is written and updated by users; e.g., Wikipedia.

Window envelope – An envelope die cut so that the name and address printed on the order form show through. The cut window is sometimes covered with transparent material.

Word of mouth – When satisfied customers tell others how much they love your products and services without you asking them to do so.

WordPress – A content management system used by people and some small companies to build their websites.

X

Xerography – A technique using electrically charged particles of pigment to reproduce images on paper.

XML (extensible markup language) – A language used by developers to define website elements and content, including text, audio, and visual.

Y

Yellow pages – The section of a telephone book, printed on yellow pages, listing businesses.

YouTube – Social media site where you can post and comment on videos.

Z

Zero-party data – Data that a customer willingly and deliberately shares with a company.

ZIP – Zip code is an acronym for "zone improvement plan." The name was intended to mean zippy or quick. The five-digital zip code was introduced in 1963 to make mail get to its destination faster.

Zip code analysis – Doing a marketing test to see in which zip codes prospects respond to your offer best.

Bibliography

Al Ries and Jack Trout, *The 22 Immutable Laws of Marketing* (HarperBusiness, 1993).

Bob Stone and Ron Jacobs, *Successful Direct Marketing Methods* (McGraw-Hill, 2001).

David Foley, *Compendium of Direct Response Terms* (First Choice Book, 2014).

Ed Nash, *Direct Marketing: Strategy, Planning, Execution* (McGraw-Hill, 2000).

Flint McGlaughlin, *The Marketer as Philosopher,* 2019.

J. Steven Kelly and Susan K. Jones, *The IMC Handbook* (Racom, 2012).

Stan Rapp and Tom Collins, *MaxiMarketing* (McGraw-Hill, 1987).

Tim and Chris Beachum, *Internet Marketing Dictionary* (4th Generation Communications, undated).

About the author

Bob Bly is a freelance copywriter with over four decades of experience, specializing in direct response and business-to-business marketing. He is the author of 100 books, including *The Copywriter's Handbook* (St. Martin's/Griffin) and *The Elements of Business Writing* (Pearson). McGraw-Hill calls Bob Bly "America's top copywriter," and he was AWAI Copywriter of the Year. His copywriting clients include Newsmax, Intuit, Uniscience, Embraer Executive Jet, PSE&G, EBI Medical Systems, Praxair, Grumman, IBM, and dozens more.

Bob has written over 100 articles for such publications as *DM News*, *Target Marketing*, *Business Marketing*, *Writer's Digest*, *Bergen Record*, and *City Paper*. He has given talks and seminars to dozens of organizations, including IBM, Thoroughbred Software, International Tile Exposition, Independent Laboratory Distributors Association, Society for Technical Communication, and Business Marketing Association.

I do have a favor to ask. If you know of a term we have omitted, please let me know so I can include it in the next edition. You can reach me at:

Bob Bly, Copywriter
31 Cheyenne Drive, Montville, NJ 07045
Phone: 973-263-0562, Fax :973-263-0613
Email: rwbly@bly.com
Website: www.bly.com